BUSTED IN BLOOMINGTON:

A Tragedy in the Summer of '68

By

Greg and Candy Dawson

First published by Dog Ear Publishing
4011 Vincennes Rd
Indianapolis, IN 46268
www.dogearpublishing.net

ISBN: 978-1-4575-5737-8

This book is printed on acid-free paper.

Printed in the United States of America

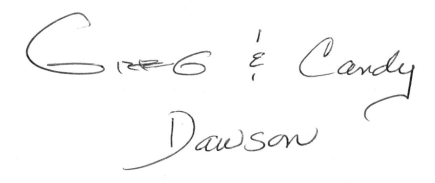

Greg & Candy
Dawson

Maitland, FL — local authors

DEDICATION

To all the English teachers

gregdawson2@me.com

candydawson@me.com

TABLE OF CONTENTS

AUTHORS' NOTES

This is a collective memoir based on interviews with over a hundred people connected in some way to the events and central figures in the story. We have not invented scenes or recreated dialogue. All the names are real. Three contacts requested anonymity, and we use the third person when quoting their words. There are some conflicts in people's memories of the same events, which is to be expected after 45 years. The narrative is based not only on those interviews but other sources including personal letters, diaries, police files, newspaper accounts and yearbooks spanning the years from 1961-1968.

I was a student when Chuck Walls, the main character, taught English and journalism at Bloomington (IN) High School from 1966-1968. I was not in his class but we were hallway acquaintances with a shared interest in journalism.

    - Greg Dawson

Greg and I met in my home state of Florida but moved to Bloomington, IN, to raise our children from 1977–1984. After we both retired, one of Greg's friends from high school, Bruce Remak, reminded us of the outlines of the story of Chuck, Myriam and Tony. The newspaper files and the class yearbook drew us in to find out more—much more, thanks to the generous, and often eloquent, memories of so many. Baby boomers do indeed remember the sixties.

Chuck Walls died long ago and Myriam Champigny (living in Switzerland at age 96) declined to speak with us, sending word from her caregiver that, "This period is a very painful one for her and if she could answer, I think it wouldn't be a good idea to remind her of it." But then there is Tony Solomito. Still living in the area and agreeing to speak with us several times, he is the one my teacher-heart went out to from the very beginning. He was thrust into adult circumstances and a spotlight no fifteen year old should have had to endure.

~Candy Caldwell Dawson

**Greg Dawson
BHS Class of '68**

**Candy Caldwell
FBHS Class of '66**

INTRODUCTION

This is a true story about coming of age in America in the '60s, about the loss of innocence and earnestness and a belief that the better angels of our nature would help us shape a "newer world" in the words of Robert F. Kennedy.

The story takes place in Bloomington, Indiana, my hometown, but it could have happened, and with slight variations surely did, anyplace in America where the baby boom generation was finding its way.

We were all buffeted by the same centrifugal forces of societal change. We were subject to the same avalanche of seismic events. We were listening to the same music.

It was, as Simon and Garfunkel sang without irony, "A time of innocence." An innocence so pure—an afterglow of the American post-war reverie —as to be untranslatable to later generations growing up too fast in more brutish times.

The central events of this story unfold from the summer of 1967 to the summer of 1968, the fulcrum of the '60s, when America swung from the Summer of Love to an early winter of sorrow and crushed hopes.

This is not the story of those in the spotlit vanguard who tripped out on acid in Haight-Ashbury, marched on the Pentagon, occupied university buildings, sat in the path of Dow Chemical recruiters, were bloodied in the streets of Chicago and the jungles of Vietnam—the iconic images that came to define "The Sixties" as we know it.

This is about the rest of us who never went to the barricades, who watched from the sidelines. We were no less transformed than our brothers and sisters in the arena, but we were disguised to our elders, and perhaps to ourselves, as agents of the status quo.

You can find us in yearbook photos of the Class of '68, suspended in time. Smiling, untroubled faces of girls with flip hair styles and close-cropped boys in coats and ties and not a whisker of facial hair. You see no hint of the turmoil unfolding outside the frames of these still-life portraits.

There is a Stepford uniformity to the pictures, not just in my class of 450 at Bloomington High School in southern Indiana, but across America from New York to Wichita, Oakland and Fernandina Beach, Florida, where my wife Candy grew up. It's as if an entire generation had been hermetically sealed in the moment by adult authorities desperate to stop the march of time and the dawning of an age they did not understand.

All yearbook portraits have a surreal, waxy perfection, but there's a heightened unreality to these photos made, per custom, in summer before the start of school. By the time our *Gothic* yearbooks were delivered in May '68, America was convulsed by assassination and riots at home and spiraling body counts in Vietnam. Our halcyon smiles of summer are jarringly out of sync, out of time.

This is a chronicle of that fulcrum year told through the life of a young teacher, Chuck Walls, who led a small band of students on a journey of self-discovery which began in euphoria and ended in tragedy, mirroring America's descent into darkness.

In his last *Gothic* photo ("Mr. Charles Walls - English, journalism, News Bureau and *Optimist* advisor") he was 23 but could be mistaken for one of the seniors. Slim, porcelain-skinned, clear-eyed, he radiates a choir-boy wholesomeness. Only neatly combed bangs, a la early Beatles, and sideburns creeping below the earlobes betray the iconoclast at work. His techniques, never before seen at BHS, pushed his students to think in bold colors outside the lines of their sheltered lives.

Chuck played Simon and Garfunkel records in class and assigned essays analyzing the lyrics. He reserved time for students to write in a daily journal. He used books considered subversive, telling students to hide their copies of *One Flew Over the Cuckoo's Nest* or *Brave New World* inside the covers of a textbook if an administrator walked in.

He broke up the military rows of desks in his classroom and arranged them in egalitarian semi-circles. Every day students arrived to a provocative new quote on the blackboard meant to unsettle and inspire. He gave extra credit for seeing movies like *The Graduate* and *Dr. Zhivago*. While overseeing *The Optimist*, the student newspaper, Chuck opened the pages to politics, debate over Vietnam, arts reviews, radical essays, short stories and haiku. He was an unabashed romantic who often began his florid, highly personal yearbook inscriptions with quoted lines of poetry and song lyrics.

"What a time it was...a time of innocence...a time of confidences," he prefaced one note.

"Last year, and even last summer, I didn't know you. This year has brought so many unexpected joys, hassles, and bits of anguish. Adding you to my consciousness has been one of the high points. I think sometimes we learn more outside the classroom from each other. There's more to say, but feelings transcend words. I will miss you. Chuck Walls."

Students were entranced by Chuck, thrilled by his illicit intellect and challenging of norms, flattered that he spoke to them, almost conspiratorially, as equals. "We were in on the ruse," said one. "He had us at hello." But there was unease, too.

To Anne Schmitz, the daughter of an Indiana University professor, "He was like a changeling, not quite adolescent and not quite adult. It was almost like he was a new breed of person. He clearly was searching for meaning, even more than we were, which made him a strange person to know as an adolescent. It's like he wasn't jelled. I think that's what made him so attractive to us. We could see the struggle and the search for meaning. We understood the pain."

Al King understood better than most. Gay and deeply closeted like his teacher, Al saw through the ebullient classroom persona. Chuck "was one of the loneliest people I had ever seen in my life. It just emanated from him how lonely he was."

It was the piercing loneliness of being a gay man and school teacher in Indiana in the '60s, when there were no "gays," just fags and queers, that led Chuck to flout the taboo against fraternizing with students. He compounded the trespass by smoking dope with them, behavior so reckless it suggested an unconscious wish to be caught.

After two tumultuous years at Bloomington High, Chuck had resigned under pressure and was headed west to lead the journalism program at a high school outside San Francisco. California was his dream destination, a place of kindred spirits and acceptance, fountainhead of the '60s culture that adorned his bulletin board, and home to the music that fed his soul.

In May, shortly before graduation, Chuck put goodbye inscriptions in many *Gothics*. One was for Julia Wrubel, our class valedictorian who gave a skunk-at-the-picnic commencement address that ruffled tassels across the Indiana University Auditorium and delighted Chuck.

Soon they would be leaving for opposite coasts—Chuck to California, Julia to Swarthmore College. He began his note with lines from Simon and Garfunkel's "A Hazy Shade of Winter."

Seasons change with the scenery
Weaving time in a tapestry
Won't you stop and remember me
At any convenient time?

"The world has changed so incredibly since 1966, as has my life," Chuck wrote. "One of the many differences on my consciousness has been knowing you. Too many thoughts come to mind, some of which border on the trite level of prose. Next week I will rejoice at our escape and then regret leaving a small circle of friends. But as Grace Slick advises, 'You'll be inside of my mind' on future days of splendour. Can you imagine us years from today? [signed] Chuck Walls."

Ticket to Ride

*L*ucy Darby awoke on a July morning in 1967 in Oxford, England, fully intent on reporting for class in the final week of a foreign-study program at the university. Then she got a better offer—to play hooky. It came from her chaperone, Chuck Walls, a 22-year-old English teacher at her high school in Bloomington, Indiana.

Chuck gathered a half dozen students, all free spirits and authority-snubbers he figured would be up for going AWOL from the Oxford reservation. Among them were Jim Sutton, brooding son of an Indiana University administrator and an early druggie; Scott Kragie, a cool-hand kid from Chicago who introduced the radical idea of wearing dark socks with loafers to Binford Junior High; Jana Kellar, whose creepy short story about an unborn child Walls published in the school paper; and Darby, a cheeky blonde with an irreverent streak who was never at home as a rah-rah varsity cheerleader.

"He said, 'You want to see a trial? It just happens to be...Mick Jagger,' and we all went, 'Oh, get out of here!'"

And so they did. Chuck and his merry band of escapees slipped away without a word to the other Bloomington High kids or his co-chaperone, Virginia Elkin, head of the English department who was shepherding half the BHS delegation. Elkin was 54, dowdy, with short bobbed hair, silver-frame glasses and a steely demeanor that made her look even older, "Sixty, 70, 80, 100 years old" to Rick Smith, one of her charges.

Meanwhile, Chuck was playing the hip big brother. Kathy Bogner was so envious of the fun her friends were having that she was granted permission in mid-trip to switch from Elkin's short leash to Walls' relaxed oversight and ticket to ride, if the opportunity was golden. Mick in the dock, in the flesh. That was golden.

The Stones melodrama was in its fifth month and grinding toward a denouement in the courts and tabloids when Chuck, Elkin and 20 students arrived in London in early July for four weeks of study at Oxford sandwiched between time in London and a jaunt to Paris. In February, acting on a tip from a Fleet Street tabloid, police had raided the estate of Keith Richards where they found something less than an orgy in progress. Jagger was charged with possession of amphetamines: four "pep pills" purchased legally in Italy but verboten in Britain without a prescription. Richards was charged with allowing his home to be used for smoking of "cannabis." Adding a frisson of flesh to the made-for-tabloid tableau, police discovered Jagger's girlfriend Marianne Faithfull naked, wrapped in a fur rug, which she let slip from time to time. She was ogled by police but not charged.

In late June, the Stones were convicted and sentenced. Richards got a year in prison and a fine (about $1,300 in U.S. dollars then); Jagger got three months and a fine of $500. They spent just one night in jail before posting bail, but the sentences, seen as absurdly harsh for a first offense, touched off a tempest that overflowed tea pots across England. Protestors marched to the offices of the tabloid suspected of ratting on the lads. The conservative *Times of London* mocked the punishment for "as mild a drug case as can ever have been brought before the courts." A newspaper ad signed by 65 eminences including novelist Graham Greene, two Nobel Prize winners and the Beatles demanded reform. "The law against marijuana is immoral in principle and unworkable in practice."

The Stones' appeal of their convictions was scheduled to be heard the morning of July 31 at The Old Bailey, the Central Criminal Court north of the river Thames not far from St. Paul's Cathedral and Fleet Street. It was the first Monday of the final week of classes at Oxford—seminars in English history, literature and architecture which Chuck eagerly attended alongside the students. Everyone raved about a young lecturer who took lyrics from the *Sgt. Pepper* album, released just a month earlier, and drew parallels with the works of Keats and Blake.

Chuck already was using the technique in his classes at BHS. His devotion to literature and pedagogy was exceeded only by his passion, verging on sacrament, for the music of the '60s. On the morning of July 31, there was no doubt the teacher was cutting class.

Chuck hustled the group onto an early train to London. Even with the tabloids whipping interest to a frenzy, the Hoosiers were able to score prized seats in the small courtroom's public gallery. Hundreds of curiosity-seekers and distressed school girls jammed the street outside The Old Bailey.

"I was so excited I don't remember a darn thing until we went into the chamber," Darby said. We were up in the balcony. It's not that big so it wasn't like we were real far away. I remember looking down and seeing this panel of guys in wigs. We could see their backs [Jagger and Richards]. It was different from anything I'd ever seen. It was mind-blowing."

Jagger was in gray trousers, a green blazer with white buttons, and a floral-design tie. The three justices were magisterial in white wigs and black silk gowns. Mick was alone in the dock. Richards had chicken pox and was confined to a small room in the courthouse "in order not to expose his mini-skirted fans to the disease" the press reported. Kragie recalls Marianne Faithfull rising up in the gallery in defense of her boyfriend, screaming at the justices, "He's not guilty!"

The court decided Jagger was indeed guilty but lifted his sentence with the warning that any law-breaking within 12 months would land him in jail. Richards' conviction was quashed for lack of evidence that Faithfull smoked weed in his home and he knew about it. The rulings triggered joyous screams from teenage girls in the gallery. Before releasing the Stones, Lord Parker, 67, the Lord Chief Justice of England, lectured Jagger, who had just turned 24. "You are, whether you like it or not, the idol of a large number of the young in this country. Being in that position, you have very grave responsibilities. If you do come to be punished, it's only natural that those responsibilities should carry higher penalties."

It's unlikely it occurred to Chuck at that moment that he too was becoming an idol of sorts to Darby and other students, that Lord Parker's words to Jagger carried a cautionary admonition for him—or that he glimpsed, in a fatalistic epiphany, the contours of his own fate.

And why would he? Chuck was in England, musical epicenter of the youth revolution, home of his rock 'n' roll gods, the Beatles. If you weren't going to San Francisco that summer, London was the place to be. Every day Chuck was breathing in pure euphoria. All things seemed possible. It was not an atmosphere likely to foster introspection and sober restraint.

Some who were not handpicked by Chuck for the London trial run remember the day in a different light. Peggy Pruett, a west side Bloomington kid, was an editor on *The Optimist* when Chuck was faculty advisor. "He left for the day. We were looking for him. He didn't tell me where he was going. I remember saying, 'Where is he?' They said he'll be back tonight. I look back on it and think it was really pivotal for him."

It was also another nail in the coffin Elkin had been constructing for Chuck since he joined the BHS faculty a year earlier and began pushing envelopes and challenging orthodoxy. The only proof they ever exchanged smiles was a staged photo in the Bloomington *Daily Herald-Telephone.* It ran with a story about the Oxford trip under the headline "Students to invade Europe."

Students To Invade Europe

By BECKY HILL
H-T Reporter

Two teachers and 25 students from Bloomington High School will invade England and Europe this summer for six weeks of study and travel with the American Institute for Foreign Study program.

Mrs. Virginia H. Elkin, 1200 Collinswood Dr., who is chairman of the English Department, and Charles A. Walls, 945 N. College, a first year teacher, were appointed by the Institute to chaperone a group of high school students who will attend special courses at Oxford University.

Although Mrs. Elkin and Walls will do no teaching in Europe—all instruction will be by local university staffs — their roles as chaperones will be to act as combination guardians, advisors and friends.

Mrs. Elkin, who has never been to Europe or England and says she is excited about the prospect, explained that the students who applied were screened for their ability in Egnlish.

The students, all from Bloomington High School, who are planning to go with Mrs. Elkin are Regina Ault, Kathy Bogner, Pamela Bo'tinghouse, Sharon Byers, Lucy Darby, Catherine Hoff, Jill Jones, Mary Ryser, Judy Brooks, Judith Pollock and Richard Smith.

Those in Mr. Walls' group are Janet Greer, Jana Kellar, Ilene LaFollette, Cathy Packard, Chris Smith, James Sutton, Ronald Voyles, Marcia Whitlow, Sara Zylman, Louiza Burkhart, Vernon Fritz, Nancy Hall, Scott Kragie and Peggy Pruett.

Leaving July 2 from Kennedy Airport, the group will spend three days in London, prior to going to Oxford. Sightseeing will include visiting Westminster Abbey and St. Paul's Cathedral, watching the changing of the guard at Buckingham Palace, climbing the Tower of London and attending an evening theatre performance.

During their four weeks stay at Oxford University, the groups will stay in Jesus College, founded 1571. They will attend courses especially organized for AIFS by the English Speaking Union, using tutors and professors of both the University and surrounding schools.

Their subjects will be British Literature and Modern Britain, as well as such related topics as Anglo-American relations.

After leaving Oxford, the groups will head for London, stopping at Windsor Castle and the John F. Kennedy Memorial at Runnymede.

The remaining two weeks will be spent touring France and other parts of Europe. They will depart for the United States August 12.

Preparing for Oxford. Chuck Walls and Virginia Elkin pose for newspaper photo. Travelers (clockwise from top left): Lucy Darby, Scott Kragie, Kathy Bogner, Jim Sutton. [*Daily Herald-Telephone* March 1967]

The enforced familiarity in England only served to breed deeper contempt in Elkin for her co-chaperone. Most group outings—Stonehenge, Buckingham Palace, Westminster Abbey, Stratford-upon-Avon—were by bus. Punctuality could be next to godliness for Elkin.

"I remember she was sitting on the bus one morning and he was late," said Pruett. "We were all on the bus ready to go. Everyone is looking around and saying, 'Where is Mr. Walls?' We had to wait while they went inside to wake him up because he had overslept. Mrs. Elkin was in front of me and I remember the utter disgust she had. She did not try to hide it at all. I never saw her talk to him. No interaction. She just looked at him like he was dirt."

In the spring after students had signed up for the trip (the prerequisites were a B average in English and $750) Chuck visited the homes of students to meet the parents, go over details of the six-week trip, and allay any parental trepidations. By all accounts, they did not share Elkin's distaste. Chuck had a natural ease with adults. Clean-cut with the decorum and orotund diction of his father, a Methodist minister, and the charm and open smile of his mother, he was a reassuring presence to conventional sensibilities.

The Darbys, upper class by Bloomington standards, lived in a big two-story brick house on an acre and a half. "Country-club people" Lucy called her parents. Her dad, an oral surgeon, was a southern Democrat, her mother a northern Republican. They were unsettled if not panicked by the ruptures in society and the helter-skelter change they saw unfolding on the campus of Indiana University, as it was on campuses across America.

Chuck had one foot in IU's Dunn Meadow with the war protestors and pot heads, but his presentation to the Darbys was classic Junior Achievement. "He showed brochures, he showed pictures, he explained what the academics were going to be, what the whole purpose of the trip was,"

Darby said. "He outlined it beautifully as an experience and adventure. It was the chance of a lifetime. That was the selling point for my mother." It didn't hurt that the Darbys shared Chuck's love for the Beatles. Another student's parents found him "very charming, a naif in every sense of the word, an innocent. We all kind of laughed because he was just so exuberant."

For Chuck, Elkin and most of the students this was their first trip to Europe. Without the telescoping intimacy of the internet, CNN, cell phones and social media, Marshall McLuhan's "global village," coined in 1964, was more theory than reality. The rest of the world remained at a distant, fuzzy remove. International travel was a big deal for a kid from southern Indiana in 1967.

Monroe Fritz had Walls for English. "He passed out this flier - we're going to take a group to England. That was so off my radar. I was a country kid, lived out north of town, worked all the time in farming and construction. A few weeks later I found myself signing up to go to Europe and I thought, 'What just happened here'?"

There was a high sense of portent for the Hoosier innocents going abroad. "I was a rather conservative child, son of a doctor," said Rick Smith. "For me England seemed, with the Beatles and Stones, a lot wilder territory than Bloomington, Indiana. I looked at it as a transition trip. I remember my parents saying you'll need a big haircut, so I had like a burr haircut going over."

Carnaby Street "gear," the epitome of '60s cool, hit the cover of *Time* magazine in 1966 and was rippling out to the heartland. "BHS Boys Find 'Mod' Fashion Trends Appealing. Girls go to Heathers, Hipsters and Baby Doll Look" declared a headline in *The Optimist* that fall. The story reported that boys "roam these hallowed halls in boldly striped paisley-print or polka dot shirts." It breathlessly concluded:

"From the midst of a book-laden, brow-beaten, knowledge-seeking BHS student body, a fashion-conscious, paisley-print, hip hugger generation emerges."

Not so much among the girls going to England. They still favored flats, A-line skirts just above the knee, and cotton blouses with prim Peter Pan collars—the preppy look sold at College Corner, The Oxford Shop and other mainstream shops on Kirkwood Avenue. The main drag linking campus to downtown, Kirkwood had long catered to the frats and sororities, but by '67 its clientele was transitioning from Greeks to freaks drawn to a mushrooming number of record stores and head shops.

The BHS girls looked as if they were dressing for a visit with the Queen, not Quant. When they boarded the plane at the Indianapolis airport "the parents were all there," Pruett said. "We were all told how to dress. I had on a Navy-blue suit, jacket, white shell, white heels, and that's how we were traveling to Europe."

Preparing for the trip helped distract Chuck from the fresh memory of losing his closest friend on the faculty, Kathy Brown, a gym teacher and fellow first-year teacher. She died in a horrible auto accident over spring break, falling asleep at the wheel on I-75 in south-central Georgia. The first day after spring break, still shaken by Brown's death, Chuck dropped by the teachers' lounge. Ida Medlyn, sophomore and junior counselor, was in the room.

"He came in and all the conversation was, 'Where did you go, what did you do on spring break,' blah-blah-blah. Everybody was up, nobody was being sad or anything, and Chuck had tears in his eyes. He said, 'My God, we just lost a teacher, a teacher was just killed, and none of you are talking about it. How can this be?' And with that he got up and left."

Chuck and Brown had dated during the school year, or so it appeared to some students and teachers who saw them at BHS football games and school dances. Pruett was in Brown's gym class. "She showed up at a football game with him and we were all like, 'Look, look! What a cute couple.' They were both very attractive." Not everyone took the couple at face value, noticing that on these "dates," Brown and Chuck were friendly but arms-length. They had to be careful because teachers weren't supposed to date, Brown explained to a student who asked why they never held hands.

Shortly after Brown's death, Chuck wrote a fond remembrance that ran on the front page of *The Optimist*. He recalled the night they chaperoned the French club's post-game dance. "She said it was unbearable to stand off to the side. I agreed but we both were concerned about proper images of teachers and found a dimly-lit corner to dance to the Supremes' 'You Can't Hurry Love.' Just as she decided we had gone unnoticed, [student] Susan Skirvin pointed her finger and exclaimed, 'I saw you! I saw you!' As we were leaving, one of the chaperones introduced her [Brown] to another as Mrs. Walls and she laughed over it on the way home."

There were pockets of speculation about Chuck's orientation, stoked in part by his conspicuous failure to bond with other male teachers, especially the macho types who doubled as coaches, and by his preference for befriending female students and teachers. Even some male students who liked Walls saw him as "effeminized" and "not manly." Al King, a gay student who had liaisons with straight jocks at BHS, instantly pegged Chuck as gay.

"I watched him around guys who were beautiful, studly-type guys, and he was a nervous wreck. He was trying to be the teacher, but you could see this other layer of him. It's kind of like vampires. We recognize each other. You can't hide. I can smell you."

Donnadee Blair, a young English and Spanish teacher, was a close friend of both Chuck and Brown. She knew Chuck was gay "as soon as I met him because I had gay friends, always." She was certain Brown was straight. "Their relationship was strictly platonic. I felt she accepted Chuck for what he was. I don't think she had a question in the world about being romantically involved with him. He was somebody to have fun with."

For Chuck the dates may have served a dual purpose. Wally Brazy said he slept with Chuck while student teaching at BHS in 1968. He later moved to Toronto and marched in gay liberation parades as "Sparkle Plenty" with "the pigeon of happiness" on his head. There was no sparkle in the closet at BHS.

"Back then you had to have an official girlfriend," Brazy said. "At public functions I had to find somebody to take. If you didn't show up with a girl you were in trouble." Official girlfriends, if that's what Brown was, were known as "beards."

The murmurings about Chuck's orientation were an undercurrent, too random to coalesce into material for the rumor mill. The daughter of a prominent business owner spoke for the great majority of students whose mental landscapes were devoid of any notion of homosexuality.

"I would not have had any sense of that. I don't even think that was something in Bloomington that anyone ever referenced. People in '66, '67, '68 were still freaked by the idea."

Busting cultural barriers meant joining the university crowd at the Von Lee art-house theater to see *The Graduate* or staying home to watch *Peyton Place* on TV. "It was so racy," she said. "The point is, nobody was thinking about people being gay."

Except for knee-jerk harrumphing from stalwarts like Elkin and a few raised eyebrows in the front office, Chuck's first year at BHS had been a great success. He earned praise from colleagues for his energetic and innovative techniques. Don Beaver, a famously acerbic history teacher, thought so highly of Chuck's methods he sent student teachers to observe his class. In just one year, Chuck had won the devotion of a remarkable number of his students including Kellar. He wrote in her *Gothic*, "Jan—It's been a good year. I'm sorry to have made it so grueling, but you pulled through OK, didn't you. I'm looking forward to next month in London, and especially to Oxford and nearby towns. See you then. Chuck Walls."

July 2, 1967, at Weir Cook Airport in Indianapolis, the BHS students and their chaperones climbed rollaway stairs from the tarmac to an airliner bound for the trip of a lifetime. A gaggle of parents waved goodbye from the windswept roof of the terminal. The students never looked back. Upon arrival at LaGuardia the travelers were informed that due to bad weather in New York their flight to London would depart from Philadelphia.

"It was nighttime and we were all tired after a long day of flying, taking a bus tour of Manhattan—the highlights were the Bowery and Chinatown where I bought a large bag of meringue tops—and then going by bus to Philadelphia to catch a late plane to London," Kragie said.

"I was sitting behind a girl I had dated and reached around her seat back to fondle her. While engaged in that merriment, I felt a very gentle stroking of my leg. I was like a deer in the headlights with a paw in the girl's blouse. I was frightened and did not know what to do, so I decided to scrunch down and pretend I was asleep. The stroking ceased as if it had never happened. My response was to stay away from Chuck for the rest of the trip."

That is, until the morning a few weeks later in Oxford when his ever-exuberant chaperone came knocking at the door with a ticket to joy ride he could not refuse.

All You Need is Love

*T*he seed for the Summer of Love was planted at the Human Be-In at Golden Gate Park in San Francisco in January 1967. The "Gathering of Tribes" was sort of the constitutional convention of the counterculture, but with better music and drugs than the one in Philadelphia in 1787. Allen Ginsberg chanted, the Grateful Dead rocked, Timothy Leary advised the gathering of 30,000 hippies to "turn on, tune in, drop out"—as if anyone there needed prodding.

By July, the magic of Haight-Ashbury was curdling into an over-crowded, commercialized mess, the authentic freak vibe of Golden Gate Park trampled by hordes of wannabe flower children and faux hippies from across America. The scene devolved into an enervated festival of dysfunctions, and in October the bummed locals conducted a funeral for "The Death of the Hippie." The psychedelic vitality of the summer had migrated east to a new capital—London.

The rock 'n' roll renaissance was in full kaleidoscopic flower in 1967. A new magazine, *Rolling Stone*, covered it all. The Doors, The Grateful Dead, Pink Floyd, The Jimi Hendrix Experience, The Velvet Underground & Nico, Big Brother and the Holding Company (with Janis Joplin), David Bowie, Arlo Guthrie, Canned Heat, Vanilla Fudge, Moby Grape, Procol Harum—all released debut albums. There were enough instant-icon songs for '67 to have its own wing in a rock hall of fame: "White Rabbit," "Somebody to Love," "Mellow Yellow," "Sunshine of Your Love," "Ruby Tuesday," "Respect," "Alice's Restaurant," "Purple Haze," "Light My Fire," "Whiter Shade of Pale," "I Can See for Miles," "Nights in

White Satin," "I Heard it Through the Grapevine," "Let's Spend the Night Together."

And there would be a separate wing just for the Beatles. They owned 1967. It began in February with release of a single, "Strawberry Fields Forever/Penny Lane," and ended in November with *Magical Mystery Tour*, a remarkable output even if the Beatles had produced nothing else all year. But it was the summer releases, including their masterpiece still taking shape at Abbey Road Studios in early '67, that secured the Beatles' preeminent throne in the pantheon of '60s pop culture.

With psychedelic serendipity, the squarely attired, neatly coiffed delegation from Indiana arrived in London on July 3 at the moment of the band's final deification: a month after release of *Sgt. Pepper's Lonely Hearts Club Band* and four days before release of "All You Need is Love." In June the band had performed the song on a BBC show beamed worldwide. The timing was magical for Chuck. The Beatles had been his artistic and spiritual lodestar since he discovered them when he was 19. His younger sister Sally remembered the day.

"We were living in Seymour [Indiana] so I must have been 9, 10, something like that. He came home one day and said, 'Come here, I want to show you something. I want to show you this album because these guys are going to be the biggest influence on music ever. Remember I said this, because they are incredible.' It was *Meet the Beatles.*"

For students who had never traveled abroad, London was culture shock. Bloomington, 50 miles south of Indianapolis, was no backwater. It was home to Indiana University, the Kinsey Institute for Sex Research, and a renowned school of music with a world-class opera program. An emerging alt music scene and hippie culture were blossoming. But it wasn't London. In the spring of '67 when Jimi Hendrix was setting fire to his guitar for the first time in a London club, Hoosiers were grooving to the smooth stylings of Vic Damone at the IU Auditorium during "The World's Greatest College Weekend."

An anti-war movement was taking hold on campus, but the status quo was hunkering down across Bloomington. During "Americanism Week," five-hundred IU students rallied in favor of the Vietnam War "to preserve the image of IU in the nation's mainstream of college students." In the city elections, all but three candidates were white middle-age men.

Chuck, Elkin and their charges stepped off the plane in London into what must have seemed a picture-book come to life. Suddenly before them were Big Ben and Parliament and the River Thames. Westminster Abbey, Buckingham Palace, the Tower of London. Piccadilly Circus, Trafalgar Square and Carnaby Street. The likes of Eric Clapton and Pink Floyd played local clubs; Paul McCartney was said to drop in from time to time.

The air was politically charged. Shouts of "Hey, hey, LBJ, how many kids did you kill today?" filled the streets. Parliament decriminalized homosexuality. McCartney gave an interview admitting he dropped acid. Two thousand people gathered in Piccadilly to protest the drug arrests of Jagger and Richards. There was a legalize-pot rally at Speaker's Corner in Hyde Park. Among the speakers were Allen Ginsberg and Stokely Carmichael, in town for a symposium on "The Dialectics of Liberation" at a converted railroad roundhouse. Student Kathy Bogner was in a group that sneaked away one night to hear a reading by Ginsberg. "We sat in the dark on the dusty floor mesmerized."

The aim of the symposium, with a roster of prominent radical thinkers including R.D. Laing, Paul Goodman and Herbert Marcuse, was "to demystify human violence in all its forms, and the social systems from which it emanates, and to explore new forms of action."

Or put more felicitously—all you need is love. *Sgt. Pepper* was the Beatles' statement for the ages. But it was "All You Need is Love" which uncannily mirrored the moment, channeling the suspension of disbelief and giddy embrace of magical thinking at the heart of the Summer of Love. The BHS students made it their theme song. It seemed to be playing every five minutes on the radio. You couldn't escape it, even if you desperately tried because it was messing with your mind.

At Oxford, 60 miles and a world away from swinging London, half the BHS delegation was housed at Jesus College, one of the colleges within Oxford University, near the center of town. The rest, including farm boy Monroe Fritz, were at Lady Margaret Hall on the River Cherwell amid acres of emerald gardens and playing fields.

"One night the guy across the hall came to see me around midnight after lights were out," Fritz said. "He told me he was afraid to turn on his radio. If the song was playing it meant he was going to die in three days. I calmed him down and said, 'Watch, I'll turn on the radio and put your mind at ease.' I turned it on and I swear the song was playing. He screamed and rushed out into the hall. I had to tackle the guy."

Paintings lined the dark oak-paneled walls of Lady Margaret—landscapes, still lifes, portraits of august personages, "people from a million years ago," said Fritz. One depicted Mary Harkness, an American benefactor of the college. Dead since 1950, Harkness was a formidable, looming presence in her portrait, a dowager in jewels and satin redolent of the oil money she married into.

One night Chuck and a group of students decided to try to communicate with her spirit using a ouija board. "I remember people in a dark room, a candle burning," Fritz said. "I have a memory of seeing something in the corner of the room. I think we convinced ourselves we were seeing Mary Harkness. It spun itself off into ghost stories and it got a little crazy for a while. Some kids got genuinely scared."

Seances, cutting class to see Mick Jagger, breaking curfew, tasting alcohol, drugs and sex for the first time. These were not part of Chuck's prim pitch to parents of the travelers. "They made a great effort to find a way to pay for this trip," said one girl. "And what they thought it was going to be and what it turned out to be were two different things."

It *was* everything Chuck promised, an "adventure" in the travel poster London of double-decker bus tours: palaces, towers, bridges, changing of the guard, Carnaby Street, fish 'n' chips, strawberries and cream, tea time. It was *Oliver* and *The Prime of Miss Jean Brodie* on stage. Basement discotheques like Samantha's, Birdland, and Whisky-A-Go-Go. A month ensconced in the groves of academe at Oxford University.

The trip was all that, but a lot more—the inevitable combustions of 16 and 17-year-olds 4,000 miles from home and parental supervision for the first time. The cloistered solitude and gravity of Oxford was like double-secret probation begging to be violated.

"The town was medieval with little of interest to us outside of the colleges and pubs," Scott Kragie said. "Social life was dominated by hormones. Weed and beer were prevalent. I was focused on drinking beer, eating Wimpy's [burgers] and chasing fellow pilgrims from New York and New Jersey. Mrs. Elkin ignored lecherous behavior toward girls from other schools."

As chaperone, Chuck was no Blutarsky but enforced a loose curfew. After a perfunctory bed check at 10 o'clock, it was don't ask, don't tell. "We had rooms on the lower floor, so we could get out of the dorm a lot, go into Oxford in the evening and hang out after curfew. And I'm sure Chuck knew," said Kellar.

"We were basically on our own," said Judy Brooks. "At Oxford they had tea for us and we tried to always be back for tea. We met some English boys and went to their houses a few times. Their parents weren't home.

We kissed a few of the boys but it was nothing serious. They took us to Stratford on Avon, the White Cliffs of Dover and Stonehenge. We sat on the stones, the tipped-over ones."

Bogner recalled the moment she knew for sure she had done the right thing by switching chaperones. "I was in the back of a coach going somewhere with Chuck's group and we were all singing along with 'San Francisco' on the radio. I'm sure Virginia Elkin would have turned the radio off rather than listen to a song about putting flowers in your hair."

Classes were held in lounges with ancient over-stuffed chairs. "We thought we were pretty important, taking classes at Oxford," said Pruett. "I remember Lucy [Darby] and some of the others would sit in class with their cigarettes lit. We were being treated like college students." And finding ways to coast like college students. "We did Shakespeare but avoided much of the reading by listening to Olivier's recordings," Kragie said. "I remember listening in the lounge. I was probably drawn by the presence of a keg of Bass Ale, the undergraduate version of afternoon tea."

Meals were served on china by college staff in large dining rooms. At Jesus College, "Tables were in long rows, with an enormous portrait of Elizabeth I tilting down from the wall, as if she were saying, 'You will eat your mushy peas and you will like them!'" Bogner said. Kragie got hooked on stewed prunes with cream. But few were enthralled by English cuisine including a venerable staple, beans on toast. Pruett, Bogner and others survived on Kit-Kat bars and Cap'n Crunch purchased at a nearby shop and Wimpy's burgers.

The weather gods had delivered an unseasonably warm and sunny summer, rendering the fields and gardens more extravagantly beautiful than ever. In the afternoons, students explored the countryside on bikes. One day when Kragie was strolling the Oxford grounds, "I heard a familiar Hoosier symphony of thumps, nets and rims clanging. I followed the sound and found a lonely American with a devastating hook shot. He was happy to have a shoot-around companion." It was Rhodes Scholar and future U.S. Senator Bill Bradley, finishing up his degree before joining the New York Knicks that fall.

The history and splendor of Oxford were not lost on the Hoosiers. At Jesus College, Rick Smith was assigned a room "right over the gate. I could look out one window and see the narrow streets in Oxford, and look out the other window and see the quadrant. They told me Lawrence of Arabia [T.E. Lawrence] had the same room. It wasn't mind-expanding like LSD, but for a kid from Bloomington, Indiana, it was pretty interesting."

"We were so enthralled with seeing everything and learning everything and doing everything and trying everything," said Darby. "We were in an old building, I mean it was like a castle. There were lead windows and we had a lookout onto the road and the little village of Oxford. Right across from our building was a bakery. It was the best bakery I had ever seen in my life. I gained 10 pounds on the trip."

For the bookish and the shy, Oxford was nirvana. "Being in seminars with people who wanted to read books and talk about them, it was truly a life-changing experience," said Cathy Hoff. "I remember a moment standing in Oxford, holding onto some rocks in a stone wall, and thinking, 'This has been here for hundreds of years.' And being in London and thinking, 'I'm walking the streets that Dickens walked.'"

The trip, sponsored by the American Institute for Foreign Study, drew students from high schools across the U.S. It was the first time BHS had sent a group. Meeting contemporaries from outside the heartland was a revelation for the Bloomington kids. They were amazed to learn that some of the New York kids had psychiatrists. There was a large gap in spending money. Most of the Hoosiers were on tight budgets. Pruett's dad gave her $150 for the six-week trip. "Most of those kids from Jersey were loaded," said Brooks. "Some even had credit cards."

Brooks, who worked the late shift at a taco shop in Bloomington to raise money for the trip, was disgusted by the heiress of a large department store chain who was drunk most of the time. "Why did she even come? We worked hard to come on this trip."

BHS students who strayed from the herd often ended up in a more sophisticated crowd. "The group of kids I hung out with were from California," said Kellar. "They thought everyone in Indiana still ate peas with a knife. They were listening to music we weren't listening to in Bloomington. That was the summer I lost my innocence. But I did not do drugs in England. I waited until I got back."

An outlier in the hipper-than-Hoosiers cohort was Sue Bradbury, daughter of author Ray Bradbury. "I was the only person from Southern California. I was real academic, didn't have many friends. I was naive in every way, real nerdy." She had never heard of Jimi Hendrix until the class with the young don who studied parallels between rock and classic poetry. Bradbury was in a group that sometimes gathered in Chuck's room for late-night bull sessions.

While his mind and door were always open to students, his soul mate at Oxford was Gail Herr, a fellow chaperone from northern Virginia. She was 30, eight years older than Chuck, a petite red-haired beauty with a sharp wit and a come-hither gaze. She and Chuck shared a love of poetry and prose and the unabashed belief that the universe bends toward beauty and justice.

"We were birds of a feather from the beginning," she said. "We always ended up doing things together with the kids because we related to them in the same way. I remember how we griped about some of the other chaperones. The kids liked me and Chuck because we weren't always on their case. We believed that you can pretty much leave kids alone. You can trust them."

Gail Herr circa 1963 [Courtesy of Laura Gail Armstrong]

Their goal as chaperones, Gail said, was "to provide an atmosphere where teenage people could feel free to love poetry and art, to explore and express their feelings, and to be kind and caring for each other"—a mantra that could have been found posted in the kitchen of any communal house in Haight-Ashbury in the summer of '67.

She saw Chuck as "a midwestern Methodist preacher's son turning hippie," an exuberant truth-seeker, an innocent. "One of the poems Chuck came across that he got very excited about was 'The Second Coming'." It seemed an odd moment for Chuck to be drawn to W.B. Yeats' dark meditation on a looming apocalypse in which "the ceremony of innocence is drowned." It was antithesis of the reigning zeitgeist which denied any possibility of existential dread.

Joan Didion mined a phrase from the poem for an essay, "The Hippie Generation: Slouching Toward Bethlehem," on the anomie of Haight-Ashbury. It re-popularized Yeats' poem and became its own mini-zeitgeist, but Chuck was drawn to the poem months before publication of Didion's essay in *The Saturday Evening Post* in September 1967.

"Chuck had, I believe, an abstract awareness of that 'rough beast, its hour come round at last, slouching toward Bethlehem to be born,'" Gail said.

Why would a 22-year-old blissfully lost in the funhouse of his first trip abroad, in the land of his artistic gods, spend even a moment dwelling on Yeats' grim prophecy? Was his abstract awareness of that rough beast purely academic? Or was it intuitive, a shudder of wordless apprehension like something in the air that sends animals scurrying for cover?

Gail wondered if there might be a punitive hand of fate waiting to exact a terrible toll from Chuck.

"Many times an 'understanding' has flashed on in my mind, that every ecstatic moment will be paid for later because something dark and envious of ecstasy will have its revenge. People who love and spend time with poetry, especially with like-minded others, have many occasions of being transported into ecstatic realms. Perhaps Chuck suspected that something dark was out to get him."

If Chuck had any intuition of calamity in the summer of '67 it dissolved in waves of "love, love, love." Gail remembered that summer as "a time of unspoiled beautiful landscapes, beautiful towns, and beautiful people. A sizable subculture of us was convinced that good ideas, beliefs, and deeds could make the world more just and more kind, something we wanted as much as or more than our own personal happiness. Life felt at times like being in a loving wonderland."

The Dangling Conversation

N one of his classmates at Seymour High School or the guys in his dorm at Indiana University can remember Chuck Walls dating. He did go to his senior prom with a girl from one of the three Jewish families in Seymour. Both were prodded by parents into going, and there was no goodnight kiss. The only other sightings of Chuck on a date were the few times he appeared with BHS gym teacher Kathy Brown at football games and school dances where they maintained a chaste distance between them.

Yet Gail remembers the man she met and fell in love with in England as a born romantic. She cast Chuck as a Byronesque figure in her fantasy of antique "courtly love" which unfolded in the Elysian fields and gardens of Oxford in the summer of 1967.

"You must imagine two young English teachers, enraptured with the magic of words and the splendor of all their uncountable possible arrangements, becoming acquainted over the pages of a poetry book while sitting on the grass beside a river on sunny days in Oxford, children playing nearby and laughter everywhere. One gets to the meaning of the poems in their deepest sense; their sense then transcends the sense of prose, and minds join on a very transcendent level."

Theirs was a torrid platonic love affair, a charming anachronism in the summer of free love and rampant random couplings. It left Gail fulfilled, not the least frustrated.

"He was a virile, tall, good-looking man with great charm, and I was pretty and petite with long auburn hair that women envied, and we never made love. We were at times physically affectionate, but in gentle, tender ways. We had so much joy—ecstasy—in being friends of the moment in one of the world's grandest places that we, certainly I, never considered a sexual tryst."

It can be said with even greater certainty that neither did Chuck. Maybe it was Gail's robust regard for her own gravitational pull on men that blinded her to the possibility that he wasn't wired for that. But entertaining that notion would have tarnished her fairytale of courtly love. Besides, Chuck was so good at playing the role of noble knight to Gail's fair maiden.

"Chuck treated me with a respect close to reverence. A thing he had, a gift of the sixties to anyone willing to accept it, was a lack of embarrassment or awkwardness about speaking of tender, exalted, loving things in a loving, tender way. None of that 'aw shucks' posturing, but rather a total poise and gentleness that women crave. Chuck would tell people in tender ways how he felt about them and how terrific they were."

He would recite lines to Gail from a poem by Adrian Henry.

In the Midnight Hour

I remember your eyes coloured like the autumn landscape
walking down muddy lanes
watching sheep eating yellow roses
walking in city squares in winter rain
kissing in darkened hallways
walking in empty suburban streets
in the midnight hour

Another gift of the sixties was the sexual revolution. It liberated a generation to sample unorthodox relationships and emboldened women to indulge, without shame, cravings of the non-ethereal variety, as men had for eternity.

"It's hard to explain certain things to those who did not 'live' the 1960s," said Gail. "It was OK and normal to love more than one person. One could be, as I was, 'in love' with two people and lovingly attached to a third person [Chuck]."

Gail left behind in Virginia a long-term relationship with a man she expected to marry someday. In England, shortly after bonding in spirit with Chuck, she fell hard in every way for an Englishman, Richard, "a tall and beautiful young man" with "long-lashed sapphire-blue eyes" and a poetic sensibility. Gail kept seeing Chuck as well and felt no pangs of "cheating." She figured he was doing the same, pursuing a separate love agenda.

"He could compartmentalize. So could I. I knew that a good-looking man in his early twenties would sleep with lots of women and I knew he loved me no less. The casual sex didn't matter. Chuck knew that I had a sexual relationship with one man [Richard] and that mattered to him little or not at all."

Even minus sexual infatuation, "Chuck probably was the best friend I ever had," Gail said. "We adored the same things: social justice, the best poetry, many kinds of music, laughter, walking and cycling and, always, the kids." Like him she knew the thrill of "enabling a student to crawl up through a poem to the 'Aha!' moment." And she shared with Chuck the common experience of an American childhood.

Gail grew up in Greenville, South Carolina, "in a somewhat Victorian home. Victorians are very big on order and stability and decorum." So are Methodist ministers in Southern Indiana. "I can't recall Chuck ever uttering swear words," Gail said. "I was the one capable, on occasion, of a foul mouth." Her upbringing also meant "Victorian expectations of what a lady should be. And I was raised as a racist." She resisted both expectations.

"Many or most little Southern girls were in some ways versions of Scout [in *To Kill a Mockingbird*]. We wore overalls all winter and were barefoot April through October. We couldn't wait to shed our shoes and go sloshing through mud and pools of water. We threw rocks, climbed forbidden trees, and issued and accepted dares."

The little girl in Gail who loved a dare relished Chuck's cheeky nighttime raids to steal sugar from the Lady Margaret dining hall for iced tea. "He eventually got caught by one of the workers who indignantly referred to 'that ginger-haired man' who came at night for their sugar." She laughed at his insistence on wearing an old dark raincoat most of the time, even indoors for his nocturnal sugar runs.

During the four weeks in Oxford their paths and interests would often diverge. "The theater for me, the Mick Jagger trial for him. Wine and beer for me, marijuana for him," Gail said. "Chuck and I never smoked together. I would not have wanted to get in trouble in Oxford. People in 1967 were very aware that kids were attracted to certain drugs and they were making rules about it. Some of the kids told me they indulged with Chuck. He never invited me. I guess he figured I wouldn't do it."

It was a rare drawing-of-the-line for Gail whose reflex, like Chuck's, was to push back against "people who wanted to make kids or anyone else march in lockstep." While a teacher at Wakefield High in Arlington, Virginia, "I would be called into the office every now and then. Once I was called in because of the way I dressed— like the kids." But unlike Chuck, the natural kinship she felt with students stopped short of her joining them in breaking drug laws. In that moment, a latent *in loco parentis* awoke in Gail, an instinct undeveloped or non-existent in Chuck.

Gail finally discovered a chink in Chuck's knightly armor near the end of the Oxford sojourn. "Like other males of that time he failed to see the blemishes in himself with regard to women. He loved me heart and soul but would not visit me when I was briefly ill. He told me, 'I didn't know how you'd look. I didn't want my illusions shattered.'"

Gail was caught up in her own illusions, on a theatrical scale. One day she was part of a group that acted out scenes from *Alice's Adventures in Wonderland* in the Oxford gardens and courtyards where the real-life Alice lived and Lewis Carroll (C.L. Dodgson) wrote the story.

"I was Alice in a pink frock on that sunshiny July 26 afternoon when the mean Red Queen began getting her comeuppance thanks to the Hatter and the March Hare. We ended with a tea party at Jesus College and I left when the Hatter was trying to put the Dormouse into a teapot, saying, 'At any rate I'll never go *there* again. It's the stupidest tea party I ever was at in all my life.'"

An illusion Gail never relinquished at Oxford was the fantasy that Chuck desired her. "He was an optimist, he was young and naive, he thought that somehow he might win. He never gave up hoping I would change my mind, part with R.P. [in Virginia], and join with him."

Why else, she asked, would Chuck quote to her the lines from a Simon and Garfunkel song, "Can you imagine us/Years from today/Sharing a park bench quietly?"

"Chuck's family knew full well how in love with me Chuck was," Gail said. "You couldn't miss it, the way he looked at me. The way, whenever it was possible, he would get close to me. Everybody knew it."

Chuck, of course, had his own unspoken reason for fostering the illusion. "My mother had pictures of them at Oxford," said Chuck's sister, Sally. "My dad once asked Chuck, 'Have you ever met anyone you think you could marry?' And he said, 'I could marry Gail.'"

As their time in Oxford was winding down, with the countryside at its most resplendent, Chuck and Gail journeyed south and west down the Cornish peninsula toward Land's End. In Devon, or maybe it was Cornwall, they ate scones and clotted cream, Gail said.

"In a darkened room somewhere, we slow danced to 1950s songs we both knew like 'Stranger in Paradise.' Chuck refrained from ever putting me on the spot, but I knew sometimes when we slow danced that he wanted to ask, 'May I have this dance for the rest of my life?' You almost did, Chuck. But not in the way you or I would ever have imagined."

"Well, that was money well-spent"

After a month of intellectual stimulation in the rarefied air of Oxford, the BHS students and their chaperones decamped to London then Paris on the final leg of their journey with simpler pleasures of the flesh in mind. One of the chaperones anyway.

The first night in Paris, Chuck arranged for tickets to Folies Bergere for "a bawdy musical farce that featured bare breasts on trapeze swings," Kragie said. "Mrs. Elkin was there, too. I was not sufficiently empathetic to appreciate her predicament."

She could either accompany her eager young charges to the notorious fleshfest, averting her gaze from the corrupting spectacle, or rule it off limits and become the grinch who stole Christmas in July. As it turned out, for many students, sitting fully clothed at the Folies was a tame prelude to their own offstage show. They had brought with them to Paris a Hoover dam of pent-up desire for action.

"The very last night in Paris, we all had a bunch of wine and everybody was getting drunk, and couples were having sex," said Rick Smith, who had occupied the Lawrence of Arabia room at Oxford. It was the first time he was ever drunk. "You were meeting a lot of young people from everywhere with their hormones raging. Everybody was hooking up because it was your last night, you're going back to your parents, you're going back to America."

"There was wine flowing like crazy at the hotel," said Bogner. "I remember walking out of my room and one of girls was passed out on the floor in the hall. Somehow, everyone was well enough to crawl on the plane the next day."

In the days leading up to the farewell blowout there were boat rides on the Seine and visits to the historic tourist icons—the Eiffel Tower, Arc de Triumph, Montmarte, the Louvre, Versailles. They provided snapshots for the photo albums which would assure parents that their children had spent their time exactly as they would have (yawn), on the straight, narrow and sober.

They boarded the plane for home bearing gifts. Bottles of Guerlaine Shalimar from the perfume district in Paris. French champagne. Ink drawings by artists at Montmarte. Wedgwood jewelry from London. A croquet mallet. Carnaby Street signs. "We really weren't flower children," Brooks said. "We wanted some objects to bring back."

They were returning to a homeland where the "Summer of Love" was little in evidence, a mirage fast vanishing in the inferno of a long, hot summer. In the six weeks the Bloomingtonians had been gone, race riots had erupted in Newark, Detroit and other places, killing dozens. Nearly a thousand American soldiers were killed in action in Vietnam. One day in Paris as the students boarded the tour bus outside their hotel, they were surrounded by sign-waving protestors shouting "Go home Americans!"

"I remember Chuck kind of laughing it off. 'Oh, it's a slow day. They don't have anything else to do.'" Darby said. "It's the most ludicrous thing I'd ever been through. I'm going, 'Are you serious? Why are these people picketing our bus?'"

The answer would become evident in the coming months as the U.S. body count spiraled to nearly 12,000 for '67, the deadliest year of the war for Americans— until the next year. It was also clear that for most of the students, and one of their chaperones, the time in Europe had been transforming, for better and for worse. It was like the cover of *Abbey Road*, thought Rick Smith. "You take four kids dressed conservatively as they go across the street and they come out like Sgt. Peppers on the other side."

"We definitely wanted to get off that plane looking different," Brooks said. "I had a mini-skirt, kind of a color block with a lot of purple in it, short sleeves, all in one piece, and it was very short. I had on black patent leather shoes, heels, with some purple on them. We had all plucked our eyebrows about bald."

The steps from the cabin to the tarmac at Weir Cook Airport served as a fashion show runway with the returning girls modeling Carnaby Street gear for unsuspecting relatives. Brooks was followed down the steps by her best friend Judy Pollock.

"My dad says, 'Well, I don't see her. Do you see her? Mr. Pollock goes, 'Where's Judy?' Then all of a sudden they recognize these two girls with super-short dresses. My dad says 'Oh...My...God.' What happened to her while she was gone?"

Darby, too, had chosen a purple mini-skirt for homecoming. As she made her way down the steps, a bottle of champagne in each hand, "My dad goes, 'Oh my God, she's wearing a mini-skirt,' and my mom goes, 'and she's carrying something.' And I was like just *waving* it. I'll never forget him looking at me in my purple mini-skirt and handing him two bottles of champagne. He said, 'Well, that was money well spent.'"

Kellar returned with platform shoes and pantyhose "neither of which existed in Bloomington at that time," she said. "I was very, very different much to my parents' chagrin. I had been kind of that perfect little kid up to then. I came back no longer the little kid in their eyes. I started doing drugs, getting out at night, doing all the things very common then."

Even the farm boy, Monroe Fritz, deplaned sporting "gear." Purple bell bottoms with a big purple belt. Apparently the look didn't play in the barnyard. "It didn't last after I got home."

Cathy Hoff, who communed with history through ancient stones at Oxford and walked with the ghost of Dickens through the streets of London, returned knowing her career path. English professor.

Jimmy Sutton brought back a Sgt. Pepper-esque jacket with a Nehru collar, a red British army jacket, and a brown bottle of clinical-grade LSD.

Kragie carried two bottles of Shalimar, a phony accent, and memories of that nighttime bus ride to Philadelphia next to Chuck. "The return to B-town was culture shock, especially for those of us who developed British accents. Chuck and I were cordial after that but had little contact. Mrs. Elkin never spoke to me again. I was a changed boy. I gave up football and went out for golf."

Bogner, who waited tables at Howard Johnson to pay for the trip, "wasn't the kid my parents put on the plane six weeks earlier. The kid who got off the plane was wearing chunky-heeled shoes, a short skirt and smoked British cigarettes that were pretty awful."

Smith brought back altered musical tastes. "Simple conservative kids like myself made a transition. All of a sudden we got out of little rural Indiana and saw the world we'd been hearing about. You felt different because you'd been to Europe, you'd been to where the Beatles and Rolling Stones started. When I got back I was much more into rock 'n' roll, Cream and different groups."

When they left Indiana, Pruett said Chuck looked like his *Gothic* picture, the minister's son scrubbed and dressed for church. "When we got off the plane he wore bell-bottom pants, plaid, I think, and a double-breasted jacket with big collars. His hair was kind of red, he let it grow, and he had long sideburns. He had the whole George Harrison thing going on."

Pruett said her mother was "mortified" at what she had going on. "I got off the plane 15 pounds heavier, my hair was a mess, I had on a

Chuck Walls and English friend at Oxford 1967

mini-skirt and chunky heels. The parents look over and see Chuck, and it was like, 'Oh good lord, what have you done?'"

At first sight on homecoming, parents like hers experienced buyer's remorse for approving the trip, Darby said. But there was unknowing wisdom in letting them take flight.

"They were all going, 'What have we done here?' And you know what? They did the right thing because our junior year was much better. I came back and I was kind of a changed soul. I was not the same girl."

Virginia Elkin was. No one recalls her stepping off the plane in chunky heels or a purple mini-skirt. If nothing else, she brought home stories for the administration and the school grapevine about the behavior of her co-chaperone.

The Sound of Silence

*C*huck began the 1967-68 school year, his second at BHS, with a promotion. He was named editorial advisor of *The Optimist*, the student newspaper accustomed to offering stories with headlines like "French Club to Dine At Chez Jean's April 2," "English Department Adds Programs," "Juniors Finally Receive Class Rings," "BHS Contributes to United Fund Drive," and "Are You a Girl or Boy," an earnest look at the issue of hair length.

A regular feature, "Did You Notice," asked if students noticed..."all the lollipops that have been eaten during and between classes...Sam Reese balancing a cane on his nose while walking down the hall...the peanut butter sandwich stuck to the wall in the cafeteria...Sonya Stuckey's monkey impersonation...the beer can hanging out of a locker on the 2nd floor, Pabst Blue Ribbon if you're wondering...red paint wearing through on the northeast stairway...the writing all over Chris Simpson's locker...the grass growing in the library planters...all the people getting contact lenses."

Editorials tackled issues such as discrimination against students unable to sit in the main booster section for a basketball game because tickets were sold out, relegating them to a section next to adults, cheerless. The cheerleading squad was admonished for staying in front of the main booster section the entire game even though the exiled students "did not have any less school spirit. We feel that these people should have had an equal opportunity to cheer the team."

For years the aptly named *Optimist* had been under the risk-averse super-vision of William Gosser, an avuncular figure who doubled as advisor and chief bottle washer in getting out the *Gothic* yearbook, an enormous task requiring worker-ant stamina. In 1965 when BHS moved from a three-story brick building on Second Street to a sprawling limestone edi-fice on the south edge of town, Gosser piled more projects on his plate.

"I was interested in getting a photo-journalism class started and I was also interested in expanding the publication ideas for kids in both *The Optimist* and the *Gothic*," Gosser said. "All the photo-journalism and *Gothic* classes filled up and there was nothing to do but hire another teacher."

Chuck was the logical choice. At IU he wrote for the *Indiana Daily Student* and did his student teaching at BHS under Gosser and an English teacher, making a favorable impression. Gosser was impressed with Chuck's work ethic. "He was always a very energetic-type person who wanted to move ahead and do things all the time and was busy" like Gosser himself. "He did a good job as a student teacher. I didn't have any problem at all with him."

Gosser, 42, was a natty, handsome man, but like many male teachers at BHS his bearing and square cultural baggage made him seem older than his years. He viewed Chuck as an emissary from planet Youth. "He rep-resented the 'Now Generation,' so to speak. He didn't seem to have much love for older-type things. He was looking ahead to the modern-day stuff. He also was very taken about that time with—what was the group from England? The Beatles."

But the cultural gap was a non-issue for Gosser because otherwise Chuck was squeaky-clean, non-threatening, adult-friendly. In the photo he included with his teaching application he's in a dark suit and narrow dark tie; his short hair is combed to the side, high on the forehead, and he wears a bemused half-smile. "The Dickie Smothers look," his sister Sally called it.

Applicants were required to submit an autobiography in their own handwriting. Chuck told of his love for movies and books, competing in Latin contests, and his involvement through the Masons (his father was a 32nd degree Mason) with DeMolay, a leadership society for young men. His graceful essay impressed the teachers and administrators who interviewed him. But he seemed so young, younger than his 21 years, that one teacher worried he was not equipped to deal with high school students and should be teaching 12 and 13-year-olds in junior high.

The concern was brushed aside and the board approved Chuck's appointment in June 1966, noting, "He has been very active in student affairs, Indiana University Foundation, etc., during his college days. Mr. Walls comes to us recommended by many outstanding Bloomington citizens as a young man of fine promising achievements." He was everything a parent might hope for in a son-in-law.

Chuck was hired to teach English and photo-journalism while serving as editorial advisor to *The Optimist*, with Gosser retaining responsibility for production and advertising. But in practice, the title was mostly titular. Chuck's name was not on the masthead and there was little evidence in the pages of *The Optimist* that someone with a fresh perspective was exercising editorial judgment.

Bogner, a senior, was *Optimist* editor that year. She thought Chuck "was lying a bit low, trying to get the lay of the land and not make waves. I went to him for advice a good bit and Mr. Gosser did not like it. He never said anything but I got plenty of stink eye. It was easy to see how he felt about Chuck. There was a room connected to the journalism classroom where we did set-up of *The Optimist* pages. Glue, scissors, light tables. Chuck and I would often talk in there because Mr. Gosser couldn't see into the room from his desk."

Chuck was one of 17 new teachers that fall, front-page news in *The Optimist* under the headline "Seventeen Faculty Additions Like, Praise

School." The story reported that Chuck once lived in Aurora, Indiana, and was a 1962 graduate of Seymour High School.

"Mr. Walls stresses reading the modern novel and believes the students should have a deep understanding of the work. He is also interested in journalism and music. Among the novels he is teaching this fall are *Fail-Safe* and *Lord of the Flies*. His favorite singers are Barbra Streisand, Tony Bennett, Bob Dylan, Johnny Mathis, the Supremes, the Mamas and the Papas, the Rolling Stones and the Righteous Brothers."

Oddly, the list did not include Chuck's guiding musical influences, Simon and Garfunkel and the Beatles. Maybe he forgot to mention them to the reporter (unlikely), or the story had to be cut for length and the editor preferred crooners like Mathis and Bennett to rockers. In any case, the first day of Chuck's English lit class that fall was a revelation for Scott Kragie and his classmates.

"He stood at the front of the class dressed in an ill-fitting suit. His hair was short on the sides and long on top with almost a comb-over look. He gave the impression he was uncomfortable in his clothes if not his skin. He wrote 'Mr. Walls' on the blackboard but did not say anything. Instead he put the arm down on an LP album, playing [Simon and Garfunkel's] 'The Sound of Silence.'"

> *Hello darkness, my old friend,*
> *I've come to talk to you again,*
> *Because a vision softly creeping,*
> *Left its seeds while I was sleeping,*
> *And the vision that was planted in my brain*
> *Still remains*
> *Within the sound of silence*

"After the song was over, he still said nothing for a long minute. The class was stunned into silence, no doubt the intended effect. He instructed us to write a theme on what we had heard."

Chuck was venturing out onto very thin ice. In Bloomington, in 1966, teachers did not use rock 'n' roll as an audio-visual aide. Simon and Garfunkel was something you heard on the radio, not in English class. No adult, especially a teacher, was interested in knowing what the words meant to *you*. Young colleagues in the English department were intrigued.

"I had never considered using Simon and Garfunkel as part of my teaching," said Debbie Horning. It seemed to be working. From Chuck's classroom adjoining hers, Horning heard "music, laughter, talk of engaged students."

Chuck "became one of our muses," said Jill Carraway. She told Chuck she was planning a unit on poetry for her sophomore classes and wanted to show how it suffused everyday life, from advertising jingles and folk songs to religious ritual. Chuck was so enthralled by the project, churning out ideas, that Carraway invited him to help teach some sessions.

"He came in with records galore. We had everything from Gregorian chants to folk songs and the Beatles. Lyrics, music, and sing-alongs merged with the bones of poetry: rhythm, form, terminology, metaphors, similes, conceits. Our approach was super-charged with Chuck's energy and his singing voice which was lively, unselfconscious, loud and infectious so that anyone felt drawn into active participation."

Donnadee Blair, who joined the faculty a year before Chuck and became a good friend and frustrated advisor, marveled at Chuck's leap of imagination and emulated him, up to a point.

Top row from left: Don Traub (band director), Wally Brazy (student teacher), Marshall Goss (track coach). Bottom: Donnadee Blair (English), Ida Medlyn (counselor) [*Gothic* 1968] and Courtesy of Wally Brazy circa 1968

"I thought what Chuck was doing was a fabulous idea and I began to do it in my English classes. But I didn't use the Beatles because, to tell the truth, before I was out of that environment, I didn't even get 'Lucy in the Sky with Diamonds.' Didn't even *get* it. Simon and Garfunkel was different. A lot of people understood the music. It was very soft."

Sgt. Pepper, with its psychedelica and reveling in the delights of weed, was the defining soundtrack for Chuck's metamorphosis, but its release still lay a year in the future. Simon and Garfunkel was a more prudent choice anyway for a first-year teacher. "I Am A Rock" was less likely to ring alarm bells than "Lucy in the Sky with Diamonds" which the Beatles insisted was not a song about LSD to counter the unanimous popular belief that it was a song about LSD.

It was not just the playing of records in class and the analysis of lyrics that set Chuck apart. It was the arranging of desks into arcs and circles. Oral book reports. Daily journals. Provocative quotes on the blackboard. Literary scavenger hunts.

"He was fascinating to us. Anything he did," said student Anne Schmitz. "When we were doing papers for him he had us scouring the [IU] campus for signs of the ideas that we found in books. Do you see them in cafeterias? Do you seem them in libraries? In bookstores? So we would go around the campus and search for these things and write a paper, and he was always very critical of the papers, but I think he appreciated the ideas. I think I got an A or a B."

Chuck's classroom was an awakening, both rude and exhilarating, for students who grew up in culturally conservative homes as he did. John Fleener came from "a very religious, far right background. I lived in a sheltered world, sort of like a cult church." In Chuck's class he learned it was not just OK to speak for himself, it was required.

"We really liked him because he was cool, but we disliked him because he tried to get us to think," Fleener said. "Most of us were just in school to have fun, to do standard things, and so if someone tried to get you to walk outside the box, that was a lot of work." Chuck was spoiling the fun by asking the meaning of "I Am A Rock."

"I think most of us listened to the music and the music drifts us along and you don't pay a lot of attention to what's being said," Fleener said. "He made you come up with an answer, and it wasn't an answer you had in a textbook but an answer that came out of your own head. It was difficult and I didn't like it. To me, a rock meant being alone."

Charles Moman's father was a Baptist preacher who took away his Beatles albums after John Lennon said the group was more popular than God, "which was a fact among many young people," Moman said. He was startled that Chuck treated him almost like an adult.

"It really affected me that he didn't see us as just punky little sophomore kids. He had high expectations of us and treated us like college kids. You immediately felt more grown up than anyone in the building. *Brave New World, Lord of the Flies.* I felt we were edgy with those books, like we were the only ones doing them. It's not that we were an 'underground' class, but in a way we were. We were different from all the others because we had Mr. Walls."

Chuck was the teacher "who really got me going into creative writing and really critical thinking," Moman said. The essays he did in Chuck's class were the only papers he kept into adulthood. When Moman became a teacher he emulated Chuck, using pop music in class and never talking down to students.

The solidarity between Chuck and his students sometimes grew into a bunker mentality—Us versus Them in administration—as he enlisted the students in a charade to conceal their literary walks on the wild side. Teachers in those days were free to choose books for their classes, except when they weren't. "I remember Mr. Walls telling us to put our mythology books in our desks and take them out if an administrator visited the classroom," said Heidi Remak.

Like everything else about his teaching, Chuck's grading system was unorthodox. "He evaluated students based on the number of 'points' one could accumulate," said Alan Tate. "The reading list included *1984, Brave New World, Catch-22, Animal Farm.* He gave points for attending movies like *Sound of Music* and *Doctor Zhivago*. I remember him standing on the sidewalk outside the theater taking names as we walked in. I did everything he assigned and more and collected over 2,000 points, which was an A."

Andy Mahler, brainiac son of a physics professor, said Chuck "worked harder than any other teacher I had. He prepared more. He was always trying to stimulate your thinking. We turned in something every day. He was doing far more assignments and grading and actual teaching than any of the teachers that I can remember."

Don Beaver, a history teacher stingy with praise if not wry one-liners, observed Chuck's class and admired his work ethic. "I think we were doing 70-minute periods at the time. He had something going all the time. Not like me who gave a big study period. He had a lot of interesting things. He had a method he wanted to teach and he was very good at it. The kids who liked him liked him. He was likable if you liked that kind of stuff."

That stuff was not just substance but style. Chuck's was the antithesis of stand and deliver. More whirling dervish. He had a nervous habit of raking his bangs to the side with his long fingers. He had a high-pitched giggle, Mahler said, and seemed to walk on the balls of his feet. "He was moving around the room, and the room was messy, and there was stuff stuck everywhere, and he was writing constantly all over everything and looking at you," said Pruett.

As the school year wore on, it was apparent that "Chuck was in some hot water because some disagreed with his choice of reading material for students," Pruett said. "I remember some parents came to his defense on this." The skeptics over 30, not to be trusted anyway, were outnumbered by the hearts and minds he won in the classroom. Chuck had pushed limits and tested the tolerance of traditionalists, but he had burned no bridges in his first year at BHS.

He was outwardly unchanged, evident in the *Herald-Telephone* photo with Elkin, his co-chaperone for the Oxford trip. Except for slightly longer hair swept to the side, Chuck in spring '67 appeared much as he did in the photo submitted with his teaching application a year earlier.

Out of respect for Gosser's experience or an instinct for survival, Chuck had not flexed his prerogatives as editorial advisor. Aside from his essay about Kathy Brown after she died in a car accident, and a commentary on the student election chiding juniors for apathy, Chuck's footprint on *The Optimist* in the 1966-67 school year was barely discernible. It continued to deliver all the news about BHS that Bill Gosser and administrators decided was fit to print.

"Did You Notice...how messy the halls are...Patty Wade walking up the stairs eating an orange...some of the guys need haircuts...Mr. Harvey's quotes from tea bag boxes...all the snow we've been having...Dan Sherman is growing a beard...Barb Weinberg and Mike Milan had measles at the same time...the girl who is taking automotive mechanics...WET PAINT in the cafeteria...Mr. Walls sleeping during convo."

It would be different next school year, in the classroom and in the pages of *The Optimist,* after Chuck returned from England with visions of a girl with kaleidoscope eyes.

Son of a Preacher Man

*C*harles Ancil Walls III was born September 6, 1944, a decade too early. He was a '60s soul misdirected by fate to come of age in small-town Indiana in the '50s, not a place or time conducive to the flowering of an Aquarian spirit. He graduated from Seymour High School in 1962, a child of the Eisenhower era.

In a cosmically correct universe, Chuck in 1966 would have been in junior high, a gifted, awkward kid in the last row, shot through with new urges, achingly young, naive, still forming, still a stranger to himself and those around him. Passing through high school in the late '60s, immersed in the transforming cultural tides, Chuck surely would have discovered and come to terms with whoever it was he was meant to be.

But he was born too early, frozen in time. The awakening never happened. And so in 1966, at 21, Chuck stood before his students as a first-year teacher at Bloomington High, brilliant and erratic, disconcertingly youthful, still agonizing and evolving like so many of them.

"When you walked in there you kinda understood that he was in a rough spot himself, that he wasn't a happy person," said Anne Schmitz, a sophomore that year. "For me, at that stage of life, it was kind of nice to know. I was absolutely in flux. It sort of felt like you were between two cultures. It was a peculiar time. It wasn't the '50s but there were remnants of the '50s. Our parents were remnants of the '50s. You felt you were reaching for some unknown change."

Chuck had known constant change all his life, but only in his address. From his birth in 1944 in Evansville on the Ohio River in far southwestern Indiana until he left for college in 1962, he lived in a half dozen communities where his father, Rev. Charles A. Walls Jr., was dispatched by the Methodist Church. They were sprinkled among the deep forests and hills of southern Indiana, places like Aurora, Princeton and Oakland City with fewer than 5,000 people.

In 1942, Charles "Jack" Walls was 22 and a fledgling minister when he visited another Methodist church in Evansville as a guest preacher. He caught the eye and ear of a pretty 17-year-old parishioner, Shirley Burton. "All the girls thought he was so handsome, but he only had eyes for her," said Sally Walls. They married a year later and Chuck was born the next year. Mary Beth was born in 1948, Sally in 1954, as Rev. Walls hopscotched from pulpit to pulpit. Shirley, trained as a teacher, became a full-time minister's wife. Jack Walls was an absentee father, in body and soul.

"My dad was not there most of the time. He was at church," Sally said. "Nobody was close to Dad. He had a distance from us. What he gave, he gave to strangers, or people in the church. My mother would pose us for family pictures and it just didn't feel natural. There wasn't that closeness. My dad couldn't handle an intimate conversation. It was all about, 'Did you get the oil changed in your car?' I never saw a letter that my dad signed, 'Love, Dad.' We were all close to my mom. She was the glue of everybody."

Shirley was also something of a rebel, rare in a midwest pastor's wife. Strikingly beautiful, she raised eyebrows by wearing bright blue eye shadow. She once painted the white garage door of a parsonage orange, yellow, and purple, to the consternation of many congregants. For better and for worse, Chuck inherited the rebellious streak.

In 1956, Rev. Walls was transferred from Princeton, a town of 8,500 north of Evansville, to Aurora, a community half the size on the banks of the Ohio River not far from Cincinnati. It was a place where telephone numbers were three digits and "everybody knows everybody," said John Baker, son of the town doctor. "You don't worry about police, you worry about somebody's mom calling your mom."

It was toward the end of the family's three-year stay that Chuck had an experience which would follow him in unimaginable ways after Aurora. At the persistent urging of his father, who said that being the child of a minister carried special responsibilities, Chuck had become involved as a leader with the Methodist Youth Fellowship. The MYF met Sunday nights in the church basement.

Baker was two years behind Chuck in school. Rev. Walls was his pastor. One Sunday night when he was in eighth grade, Baker visited the basement restroom during a break in the MYF meeting and was met by Chuck.

"I was using the restroom and I thought he was coming after me," Baker said. "He made a play for me. He reached for me. I rejected it and that was kind of the end of it. I never said anything to Rev. Walls and never said anything to his mother."

In the middle of Chuck's sophomore year at Aurora High, Rev. Walls was posted to First Methodist Church in Seymour, on I-65 between Indianapolis and Louisville. With nearly 12,000 people, including a budding rocker named John Mellencamp, Seymour must have seemed like a metropolis after the string of Mayberrys. The move was a promotion for Rev. Walls, but for the kids it was just another uprooting of their lives.

In the 1960 Seymour High yearbook, *The Patriot*, Chuck has the sulky stare of someone rousted from bed for a dentist appointment. Skinny and bespectacled, a portrait of nerdiness, he struggled to find his place at the school. Don Beaver, a history teacher who later became his colleague at BHS, saw it up close.

"Chuck was in my class as a sophomore. He had trouble fitting in. Seymour was a country town, more or less. The smart kids at the school were farmers. They were your best students usually. Chuck was a little different, and because he always moved around he had a hard time getting friends. I thought he was alienated. He was trying to be part of things. He even went out for cheerleading. Another boy went out with him. They were terrible."

The other boy was John Armstrong, nicknamed Cosmo, a short, husky red-head whose brother had been a sports star at Seymour. He was desperate for attention, Chuck for acceptance. The cheerleader tryouts were held in the gym before the student body. "They didn't dress up like girls or anything," said Patty VonDielingen. "They were odd, not like everybody else. People laughed at it. Two misfits. Leave it to those two to do something."

VonDielingen and Chuck became good friends, thrown together by the school's practice of seating students alphabetically, starting with home-room. "We were always next to each other," she said. "We were in the same English class for three years. Every morning he would be in the room when I got there, and he would always say, 'I wish I could give you some good morning kisses.' He passed me notes all the time. 'You are the best of everything.' 'Thanks for helping me with all the problems in February when I called you on the phone.' I can't remember what he needed my help with. I always had the feeling Chuck really liked me. But I never considered going out with him."

A few girls, sensing Chuck's isolation, went out of their way to try to include him. "I always made sure I spoke to him, to say you're in my group or in my crowd," said Marvina Schwartz. "He wanted to fit in. He worked very hard at that. He just didn't have enough confidence or self-esteem."

Even girls who liked Chuck in that way did not see him as boyfriend material. Dena Klein, a year ahead of Chuck, knew him through MYF and their families were close.

"Chuck was like another brother. Both his parents were very good-looking, but in high school he had not developed. He was tall and thin and had a burr haircut. Not the coolest guy around by far. He loved music, rock 'n' roll. One song he just loved was the 'Monster Mash.' He would get out there and dance to that. I'm so glad he didn't ask me to dance."

Chuck was rarely seen at dances or football and basketball games. When he did go he sought out the refuge of friends such as Klein or fellow wallflowers like Sharon Kilgas, who lived on the poor side of town. "All the kids wanted to be popular, but I wasn't." At sock hops, "Chuck was shy about dancing," Kilgas said. "We palled around together and danced every other dance."

Chuck didn't date. "He wasn't the kind of guy who appealed to girls," said Beaver. "He wasn't on the basketball team." And he seemed to have no guy friends except weird Cosmo and Ron Unger, who worked with him on *The Owl,* the school paper. Chuck was persona non grata in jock circles.

"He wasn't really a person me or any of my friends would hang out with," said Joe Baker, a letterman in two sports. "His actions, the way he carried himself, were feminine-acting. There's no way he was one of the rough-and-tumble type people."

Chuck's style was anything but. "He liked to come to school dressed up in a tie," said Linda Marsh. "He always looked very neat. Back then blue jeans were 'in' for guys. That was Chuck. He was just different."

And smarter. As Chuck settled in at Seymour High it became apparent that his social ineptitude masked a superior intellect. It had the ironic effect of intimidating some potential friends he so desperately wanted. "He was super intelligent," Marsh said. "To be honest, I don't know if we ever had a conversation. I wasn't on the same level with him." Schwartz, on a college prep track like Marsh, said Chuck "was so much smarter than the rest of us. But I don't ever remember thinking he was condescending to anyone not as smart."

The classroom was the only place Chuck was a fish in water. Suddenly it didn't matter that he was a central-casting geek. Gone was the flummoxed, bashful Mr. Peepers, replaced by a smart, irrepressible wiseguy. "He would speak up to teachers in class, make jokes, he *got* things," said classmate Barbara Osipe. "He was clever, witty. He would speak up to teachers in class, make jokes. It almost got to the point, 'Alright, Chuck. That's enough.'"

In the spring of his senior year, Chuck asked Osipe to the prom. It was a date made in outlier heaven. Osipe's was one of just three Jewish families in Seymour. They drove 60 miles to Indianapolis to go to synagogue. She was not thrilled with Chuck's invitation.

"I always felt a little like an outsider, not so much my Judaism as my personality. I was not asked to the prom my junior year. I was not ugly, just not in the boy-girl clique. They thought Chuck was odd, geeky. I sure didn't want to be put in the same category with him. I came home and complained. I thought it was ironic that I was asked by the minister's son. My mother was very insistent that I go. 'You need to experience prom.'"

The prom ("Southern Nocturne" the theme) was at the school and the after-party at the National Guard Armory. Chuck drove and had some trouble pinning Osipe's corsage. "I'm happy I went," she said. "Chuck and I had a really nice time. Maybe we even felt a little 'cool.'" But the starry night ended in awkwardness at Osipe's doorstep.

"I see the brown front door before us. It was daylight, probably between 5 and 6 a.m. I remember fumbling for my keys. We both must have been exhausted for having been up so long. I was concerned that my over-protective parents would come to the door or be peering out a window. I wanted to slip into the house as quickly as possible. Prom night was over, and I certainly did not want to kiss or be kissed by Chuck, and perhaps he felt clumsy about any endearing moment. So we retreated back into our molds as soon as the front door closed."

The 1962 *Patriot* yearbook reflects the final stage of Charles Ancil Walls III's three-year metamorphosis from unsmiling freshman loner to academic all-star, top 16 in a class of 220, renaissance man of school clubs: yearbook and newspaper; math, science and Latin; dramatics and concert choir; Future Teachers of America and photo club; tennis team manager; secretary of Hi-Y, motto: "Clean Sports, Clean Thoughts, Clean Speech, Clean Habits."

In the gallery of senior portraits, Chuck is in coat and tie and still has old-man-frame glasses and the buzz haircut of a plucked chicken. But in his eyes and easy half smile is a look of pride in achievement, of hard-won confidence, even a trace of happiness.

That fall Chuck enrolled at Evansville College in the far southwestern corner of the state where both his parents had studied. Evansville was a private, Methodist-affiliated college with fewer than 1,500 students in 1962. Chuck stayed one year. Not "hip" enough for him, Sally said. While there "he began his physical transformation. He grew longer hair, lifted weights and got contacts. No longer the nerd, he was ready to move to a bigger pond."

Chuck was ready to head north to Bloomington, to Indiana University, an oasis of progressive thought and growing social ferment in a conservative state where most folks were still happily rooted in the '50s. In Bloomington, Chuck's dormant '60s soul finally would breathe free. He would find kindred spirits and joy, and begin a journey from self-discovery to self-destruction.

Ascots and Undies

*I*ndiana University was on the cusp of the '60s—the era not the decade—when Chuck arrived on campus in late summer 1963 to enroll as a sophomore after a restless freshman year at somnolent Evansville College. Not that IU had fully awakened to a new day. The campus still had one foot firmly planted in the post-war era.

All male undergraduates had to take part in ROTC. Blue jeans were not allowed at mealtime. In group photos at dormitories and Greek houses, the men are in coats and ties, the women in skirts. Most men's dorms had an official "sweetheart," a lone coed in a sea of Robert Hall jackets. A fraternity invited a candidate for *Playboy* magazine's "Bunny of the Year" to its annual Bunny Dance. Drinking and drugs were forbidden on campus, and women had to be back in their rooms by 11 p.m. on weeknights, 1 a.m. on the weekend.

In the 1963-64 *Arbutus* yearbook, the tone of mainstream campus life is captured in a photo taken at a women's dorm: "After midnight, when the girls get together, the subject may be boys, bridge or differential calculus. But the discussion is sure to be interrupted a couple of times by a telephone ringing or a new folk song which prompts an entire hootenanny." Pictures from a fraternity house have the same Rockwellian vibe: "Great fun begins when brothers get together for a few minutes of basketball, a card game, a chorus or two or, in season, a snowball war."

The only hint of social unrest in 500 pages are photos of a "mass kiss-in" on Valentines Day to protest a ban on smooching in the lounge at

Sycamore Hall, a women's dorm. A herd of clueless men in winter coats huddle on the steps outside the hall waiting in vain for their kiss: "Dan Cupid was unable to attend, and nobody else seemed to know how to start the party."

Outside the pages of the *Arbutus*, the '60s era had already begun to unfold at IU. There was a budding free-speech movement on campus, among the first in America. A chapter of Students for Democratic Society (SDS) was established in 1964. But the seminal event marking the start of '60s activism at IU occurred even earlier, in October 1962, and made news across the country.

About 30 students—members of the Fair Play for Cuba committee and the campus chapter of the Young Socialist Alliance (YSA)—gathered on the steps of the IU Auditorium on Oct. 24 to protest President Kennedy's ongoing naval blockade of Cuba where the Soviet Union was deploying nuclear missiles. As the group marched toward downtown it was heckled by hundreds of counter-protestors. The besieged Cuba protestors turned back, taking refuge in the IU library. Police arrested a pizza parlor worker who struck a protestor while grabbing and tearing up her sign.

The incident became a national *cause celebre* when Thomas Hoadley, the local prosecutor who never liked the idea of a YSA chapter at his alma mater, got a grand jury to indict three YSA Cuba protestors for subversion under Indiana's 1951 Anti-Communism Act. The charges ultimately were dismissed by the courts, but not before Hoadley's political witch hunt yielded a drug arrest which made headlines across the state and triggered the war against marijuana in Bloomington.

Nancy Dillingham was a 21-year-old theater major at IU in April 1963 when she was ensnared in Hoadley's dragnet. He said Dillingham was under investigation for possible ties to YSA when a tipster said drugs could be found at her home. She was arrested after police discovered half a pound of shredded marijuana at her off-campus apartment. Hoadley claimed that Dillingham made regular trips to Chicago to pick up Communist literature and brought back marijuana from a "Chicago syndicate."

None of that was true, said Dillingham, but IU officials rushed to judgment, suspending her from classes. A year later she was convicted by a Bloomington jury which recommended a $1 fine. Her lawyer, Richard Wilder, a criminal defense attorney with a taste for combat and notoriety, persuaded the court to suspend Dillingham's sentence of 2-10 years in prison. Perhaps Chuck made a mental note of it at the time. Four years later, he would come knocking on Wilder's door.

There's no evidence Chuck had begun smoking dope when he arrived at IU. He was a tea drinker, said his first roommate, Ron Unger, who graduated with Chuck from Seymour High in 1962. "It was almost, I won't say a ritual, but a routine. Chuck was purposeful, even to the idea of drinking tea. He would do *this*, he would do *this*, he would do *this*."

Unger doesn't remember how it was he and Chuck became roommates at Wright Quad their sophomore year. They'd had no contact since graduation when he headed for IU and Chuck for Evansville. With nearly 20,000 students on campus, it was a remarkable coincidence that friends from a small town ended up in the same dorm room. Unless it was no coincidence. Unless Chuck, unbeknownst to Unger, had orchestrated it. The theory seems farfetched to a fantastic degree. But it seemed to play out for real the next year with a different target. This one, however, pulled back the curtain on Chuck's machination.

John Baker, who said he fended off Chuck in a church restroom when they were teens in Aurora, attended Culver Military Academy in northern Indiana, graduating in 1964. He and his roommate, also named Chuck, submitted paperwork to room together at IU their freshman year. Baker was startled when he heard back from university housing.

"I got this notice that said you've already requested to live with Charles Walls. I did? I told them, 'No, no, no—I didn't! You got that wrong.' So I had to go through all this stuff to get it straightened out." Baker and his Culver buddy moved into their room at Foster Quad as planned.

"I was kinda wandering around and in a room at the end of the hall was Charles Walls," Baker recalled. "He said hello, and I just said, 'Let me ask you something. What happened here? He said, 'Well, I just thought it would be fun to room with you.' I asked why he indicated to them that I wanted to do that. And that was the end of it."

But it wasn't. "One morning about 4:30 I wake up and I think maybe Chuck my roommate is up because there's somebody sitting at the desk. But I look over and Chuck's in bed. It's Charles Walls sitting at the desk, staring, and I said, 'Chuck, get outta here and don't come back. I don't want to be rude. Just go. I'm not interested in that."

After a month in the dorm Baker—headed for IU law and an eventual seat on the Indiana State Court of Appeals—pledged a fraternity, Sigma Alpha Epsilon. He spent most of his time at the frat house but returned occasionally to Foster to visit friends. Chuck was there to greet him.

"He was very bright and when I was doing my freshman comp he was very persistent," Baker said. "He would say, 'Let me help you with that.' I told him somebody at the fraternity house will help me. I finally had to say it's obvious you have desires I'm not interested in. I just don't want to go there."

"There" was a dangerous place to be in 1964. Chuck had to be discreet. "The athletes usually lived in the dorms closest to the athletic complex like Foster," Baker said. "I don't know the extent to which other people knew about Chuck's propensities, but there were a lot of football players on our floor, big no-neck guys who would eat your face for a dime, and they would have beaten up a gay."

Whether Chuck and Ron Unger became roommates at Wright Quad by amazing coincidence or furtive design, it proved to be a harmonious pairing. Per student custom they lined a cardboard box with aluminum foil and stuck it on the window ledge as a makeshift cooler. "I don't remember if we had beer in it," Unger said. "I doubt it because we were pretty straight-laced at the time."

Like most roommates they had different habits and tastes. Chuck was "a vanguard kind of guy" who liked the Beatles, Unger said. "Johnny Burnett was my taste." Chuck could be aloof, Unger said, and was concerned about being neat, even fastidious. "He had a collection of 78 rpm records and was very picky about who touched them, almost as if they were artifacts."

They didn't talk about sex and Unger never thought about Chuck's orientation. Looking back, there were confusing signals. "He had a subscription to *Playboy* magazine and I remember once he became somewhat upset when someone handled his latest issue. If he was gay, why the interest in *Playboy*? Was he one of those who claimed he just read it for the articles?"

Chuck "didn't discover who he was until his freshman year in college at Evansville," Sally said. "In high school he was a bit of a nerd and was already considering how to change what didn't please him." The process of self-discovery and the working out of identity issues continued at IU, sometimes tinged with exhibitionism that recalled his cheerleading tryout before the student body at Seymour High.

Monty McDaniel, an IU wrestler and son of the coach, lived two rooms down the hall from Chuck at Foster when he was a freshman and Chuck was a senior. "Chuck was probably one of the friendliest guys in the dorm. Always had a smile on his face. And he'd talk to you. But he was strange. He would leave his door open. His roommate was a guy who studied all the time. Every time you looked in the room he was studying.

The door was left open all the time, I assume because of Chuck. He was always trottin' around in his underwear. Tighty whities. Constantly, I mean constantly, any time that door was open, Chuck was in his undies. He would be at his desk sometimes in his underwear."

Chuck's penchant for neatness verged on germaphobia, McDaniel said. He would use a piece of toilet paper to pick up a trash can. "When he went to class he was always neatly dressed. You could tell when he was going out to meet somebody. He would dress up, almost like a leisure suit, and he would wear these scarves—ascots. I have no clue who he was meeting. He never brought anybody around. I never saw any girls in his room."

The more time and space Chuck put between himself and his life as the obedient pastor's son, the farther he drifted from his lockstep faith. "They would just nag us to death because we were minister's kids," Sally said. "Chuck was the first to fall away. He refused to be shamed into attending church. He couldn't stand the hypocrisy, people sitting in church acting holier than thou, and you knew they were treating people badly all the time. My mother would say, 'Well, there's no better place for people with problems than in the church.'"

During his sophomore year when he roomed with Unger, Chuck met Alan Thomas, a freshman living in a different wing of vast Wright Quad. They studied together that year and became roommates the next fall at Foster after Baker thwarted Chuck's gambit. Thomas and Chuck were doppelgängers of sorts, sensitive outcasts from the hinterlands still working out their identities. "I grew up in a little town, Brazil, Indiana, very repressed, very bullied," Thomas said.

One thing they didn't have in common was study habits. "When I say I went to college, I didn't really go to college," he said. "I lived in Bloomington and I kind of went to college sometimes. Peter, Paul and Mary did a concert in Terre Haute, which is about 30 miles from Brazil. Chuck and

I spent the night at my house in Brazil and drove the next night to the concert. Then the next day we had to be back for class. Of course that's a joke. *He* had to be back for class. He was really obsessed with all of that.

"We had a good time as roommates. Chuck got us into trouble the night Johnson was elected over Goldwater. He was just crazy for Goldwater. Well, he got drunk and yelled out the top window, 'Fuck Johnson!' In those days you couldn't do that. The counselor came up and said who did that? Of course we both denied it."

It would be the most pivotal friendship of Chuck's life, and another instance of the malignant kismet that seemed to shadow and guide him at IU. Through introductions made by Thomas, he would find love as a gay man for the first time and meet Myriam Champigny, a professor's wife who would provide the stage for the most consequential chapter of his life.

"I met Myriam the very first day I was at IU in 1963," Thomas said. "She was signing up people for animal welfare something or other and we became kind of friends and then we became very close friends. Myriam was the person who told me I was gay. I was at her house one night drinking wine and smoking dope. I don't know how it came up, but I said, 'Oh my God, I think I'm gay!' And in her French accent she said, 'Of course you're gay, obviously you're gay. What is the big issue here?' That liberated me."

Thomas, in turn, would be witness to Chuck's liberation; even, in a way, his facilitator.

"I was gay but Chuck and I never talked about it. Then he fell in love with a casual friend of mine, a kid named Billy. He was a hustler in Indianapolis, but I'm not saying that negatively. Billy was a really nice, sweet kid, and that's just kind of how he made his living. He lived with a prostitute in Indianapolis. He would come down to visit me. I was living in a house with three or four other people and Chuck would be there. Amazingly, all of a sudden, there was a connection. And it was a total shock to me. That was the first I knew he was gay. Billy was a prostitute but this was not about money. I think there was genuine care between them. They really liked each other."

Otherwise, Chuck had a thoroughly mainstream experience at IU, never drawn to the emerging counter-culture of "green-baggers," scruffy non-conformists and intellectuals who toted green canvas bags as badges of revolt. He majored in English, took education courses, wrote for the *Indiana Daily Student,* and joined the Union Board and IU Foundation, button-down boosters of the campus status quo. All around them the ground was shifting.

Chuck Walls (standing left) and Ray Maudlin (glasses), Foster Quad, Indiana University [*Arbutus*, 1965]

The *Arbutus*, which had so neatly air-brushed reality in the early '60s, ran out of brushes by 1966, the year Chuck graduated. On page 8 are photos of protestors with signs, "Get out of Vietnam," "Stop the Slaughter of the Vietnamese People," "Negotiation not Escalation." On the facing page are photos of card sections at IU football games spelling out messages like "DAD$," like transmissions from a distant 1950s planet. The yearbook chronicles the proliferation of campus reform groups and forums for discussion of radical politics and culture which "usually ended in toe-to-toe shouting matches." The Student Liberation Front playfully demanded a marijuana license for the student union and the complete abolition of student government. The next year Guy Loftman, an SDS leader, was elected student body president.

Like IU, Chuck was in transition. He had shed the skin of the burr-headed nerd from high school, letting his hair grow, ditching glasses for contacts and capping his teeth. He had left behind the conservative political views and blind fealty to faith learned at home. But in crucial ways the essential Chuck was unchanged, still a fearless babe in the woods.

"I was never innocent. Chuck was," said Thomas. "He just went through life always expecting the best from people, always expecting the right things to happen. I just don't think he saw any danger in anything. Chuck was an innocent, he truly was. I could have sold him the Manhattan bridge."

At Seymour High, Chuck was a member of Future Teachers of America. After four years of exposure at IU to a wider world of possibilities, he still saw teaching as his future. The pedagogic urge was deeply embedded in the family DNA. Like most preachers, Rev. Walls was a "teacher" from the pulpit. Shirley was an educator and opened the first school in Seymour for students with special needs called the Sunshine School. Sally, too, would be drawn to the classroom after success in other professions.

"His love of music and the lyrics full of messages was something he shared with others. So teaching literature was something that made perfect sense to him," Sally said. "There was no big announcement, 'Hey, I've decided to teach!' Just a quiet transition, not looking for applause."

Sally was Chuck's first student. In 1965, Rev. Walls was transferred to the Methodist church in Sullivan, a town half the size of Seymour, 60 miles west of Bloomington over two-lane roads.

"He was my lifeline because we lived in a town I didn't like at all," Sally said. "The kids were very mean to me. I hated Sullivan. He hated the fact I was going through that. He began to teach me the arts. My mom trusted him. She and my dad were so involved with the church, she kind of left it up to him to instruct me.

"He took me to concerts and films. Simon and Garfunkel. *A Man and a Woman.* My first Bond double-feature, *From Russia with Love* and *Dr. No.* He had me reading things I wouldn't normally read at a young age. *Lord of the Flies, Catch-22, Tortilla Flat, Fahrenheit 451, 1984, A Catcher in the Rye.* Maybe he knew he to had to give me a crash course just in case."

In September 1966, Chuck arrived at the future as an English and journalism teacher at Bloomington High. He told the school newspaper that one book he planned to teach was *Lord of the Flies.* He turned 22 on September 6, during the first week of school.

"I believed he looked at younger people and wanted to make an impact on them, maybe because he wanted to make their teenage years easier than his. He wasn't much older than those he taught but years wiser," Sally said, adding something Alan Thomas knew, "He was too trusting of others and unaware of the dangers ahead."

Round Peg in a Square Hole

$\mathcal{T}$he new Bloomington High School on South Walnut Avenue, which opened in 1965 in place of the aging (1914) brick palace on Second Street, is a streamlined monument to limestone mined from local quarries. The same stone was used in construction of American icons such as the Empire State Building, the Pentagon, and the National Cathedral.

It also defines nearly every building on the Indiana University campus including the Herman B Wells Library, the setting for a scene in *Breaking Away*. The 1979 movie about four working-class Bloomington kids who mount a quixotic challenge against privileged frat rats in a bike race won the Oscar for best original screenplay. In the film one of the boys, mocked as "cutters," is sitting outside the library with his father, a stone-cutter who mined limestone for the building.

"I was proud of my work," he says. "And the buildings went up. When they were finished the damnedest thing happened. It was like the build-ings were too good for us. Nobody told us that. It just felt uncomfort-able, that's all."

Nobody told Peggy Pruett the buildings were too good for her the first day of class at the new BHS. She just felt uncomfortable. "I knew the characters in the movie. I experienced the town-and-gown division."

Pruett grew up on the working-class side of the divide. People on the west side of Bloomington assembled televisions and TV parts at the RCA and Tarzian plants, ran small businesses, did blue-collar work for the city and IU, and some labored in the quarries. On the east side were the doctors, lawyers, bankers, company owners, and professors.

Children attended schools on their side of the divide: Binford Junior High and University High, a "lab" school affiliated with IU, on the east side; Dyer, Central and BHS on the west. The twain rarely met except in sports. Traveling to the other side for a rare matchup of basketball or football teams seemed like a journey to another country.

The invisible barriers came down in 1965 with redistricting. East and west finally met on the common ground of the new BHS on the south side of town. Many Binford kids who in the past would have gone on to University High were assigned there. They brought with them a larger-than-life aura. Pruett and most of her friends arrived with an inferiority complex.

"The counselors at Central felt sorry for the girls because they were going to meet the Binford girls for the first time," she said. "The Binford girls represented the east side, and the east side represented money. We had a saying that you could tell if you were from the east side: you had straight teeth because you had braces. If you were from the west side you didn't.

"We hit that sophomore year down there and we don't have much. We don't have clothes, we don't have trips, we don't have fine homes, we don't have dinner discussions about the war in Vietnam. My mom was working night shift at a factory then. There was always a divide with the Binford girls. I had a good friend from Binford who spent summers in Maine with her family. I didn't have 35 cents for Bryan Pool."

Most Binford kids came from more affluent homes with well-educated parents who espoused liberal views. "They questioned policy in Southeast Asia while most on the west side were baking cookies and packing care packages for brothers, neighbors and boyfriends," Pruett said. "Many of those serving in Vietnam did not have educational deferments because they could not afford college."

The prevailing attitude at the time, said Ida Medlyn, a BHS counselor, was that, "Anybody who was anybody sent their kids to U-School. And the others went to Bloomington." A group of prominent families whose children were redistricted from UHS to BHS responded with their own version of "Hell no, we won't go!" to the school board.

"My brother and sister went there and I knew all the teachers, so going to BHS was kind of a letdown for me," said Lucy Darby, the oral surgeon's daughter. "Our parents were willing to pay $2,000 for us to go to U-School. A lot of us fought like dogs to get to U-School and they absolutely declined it."

Darby and Pruett became sophomore classmates at BHS in the fall of '66. Darby's worst fears were realized on day one at a convocation with the assistant principal, John T. Jones, an expressionless man with a crew cut, 40 going on 60. "When he started talking it was such a different vibe than I was used to," she said. "He had a hick twang. And I thought, OMG. I'm here for four years. I have no idea where the hell this is going. It was culture shock."

Darby would look back not in anger but gratitude for the intransigence of the school board that sent her to BHS. Where the hell this was going, ultimately, was England and France with Chuck in the summer of '67. "The best moment in most of our lives," Darby said. It would be Chuck's best moment, too. But that fall the rookie teacher found himself reliving his worst days from high school, once again the outsider.

"From the very beginning when we looked at each other in the first teacher meeting, I felt he was a fish out of water," said Blair, also in her first year at BHS. "I felt that everyone including me was very concerned about Chuck because he was different. He didn't fit into the square hole. He was round. You have students like this. You see them and you know right then they are not going to fit."

Top row from left: John T. Jones (principal), Virginia Elkin (English), William Milne (assistant principal). Bottom: Bill Gosser (journalism), Bill Sturbaum (history), Don Beaver (history). [*Gothic* 1968]

Blair saw Chuck more clearly than he saw himself. He arrived at BHS with the belief that here, at last, his isolation and loneliness would end.

"When he started out he was full of optimism, thrilled that he had a peer group, a teacher peer group," Blair said. "Chuck really, really wanted a teacher support system. But it was clear to me he was not accepted by the teachers. I felt he did not have a chance with the men."

William Gosser, who supervised Chuck as a student teacher, said "it didn't seem like he had any contact or relationship or anything with the men teachers, the older men teachers. I don't remember that he even went in the teachers' lounge. His interest seemed to be with the students." He never attended English faculty potluck dinners. "I don't think he had an interest in socializing with faculty, even for drinks after work or on weekends," said colleague Karen Boswell.

Social studies teacher Bill Sturbaum was the teacher union rep and openly liberal. He was not a smoker "but if you wanted to be with teachers that's where you had to go. It had a suspended ceiling and the bars were brown from smoking. I don't remember seeing Chuck very much in the teachers' lounge." Later, rumors that Chuck was smoking dope with students became a hot topic under the nicotine-stained ceiling.

The only time anyone remembers Chuck in the teachers' lounge was that day after spring break in 1967 when he silenced the chattering with his outrage that no one was talking about the death of gym teacher Kathy Brown. When he stormed out it was confirmation, if any was needed, that the round peg was never going to fit in the square hole. The peer group he hungered for was not to be found in the lounge.

Chuck's black-sheep standing was just as evident to students. For Andy Mahler, a professor's kid and iconoclast who suffered through junior high and didn't like BHS much better, Chuck's class "was one of the brighter points of the day, just because he cared so much." Chuck's ostracism was obvious.

"You could tell he did not fit in with the other teachers, especially the male teachers," Mahler said. "I never had an inkling that he was gay. But he wasn't 'manly.' He had sort of a weepy face, and a girlish giggle. He had very long fingers, sort of manicured. A lot of the other men teachers were coaching something and Chuck wasn't. He just did not fit into the macho, jock culture."

Al King was a closeted gay student and excellent phys-ed student who avoided team sports but ingratiated himself with coaches and teachers at BHS, serving for a time as a gym-class assistant to the football coach, Fred

Huff. He was startled by what he overheard about Chuck from Huff and others.

"I was amazed how hated he was in the teacher ranks, how they castigated him. Mr. Huff had nothing good to say about Mr. Walls which was interesting because Mr. Huff hardly ever talked. He called him a damn hippie. Another coach was, like, 'You stay away from him, he's a dangerous character.' Mr. Scott, a biology teacher, a lovely man, could not bear Mr. Walls. 'He's a joke as a teacher, he shouldn't be here. I think he's a danger to our students.' I never heard Mr. Scott say bad things about anyone except Mr. Walls."

The only chance of a peer group for Chuck, it turned out, was among his true peers: students. Not just any students—those like him in temperament, maturity, musical taste and alienation from mainstream BHS culture. At 22, Chuck was only five or six years older than his students. His classroom became a port in the storm for east-side refugees of redistricting whose presence scrambled the demographics of the old school and altered curriculum.

"It did all change," said Sturbaum. "The old school was *old school*. We didn't have air conditioning. In SCAP [a social studies class for advanced students], our kids came right out of Binford, so we had all those kids from IU families. It was ungraded. We could have a curriculum you didn't ordinarily have. We read Machiavelli. *1984. Report from Engine House 76* about the slums of New York. The administration trusted us. We never even reported what we were going to read."

Chuck became an accidental Pied Piper. Some like Kathy Higgins, a Binford girl, were assigned to his English class. "He was casual in his personality, and friendly. Because he wasn't that much older than we were, it was almost as if he was a student himself." From a reading list of provocative titles, she chose *One Flew Over the Cuckoo's Nest*. "I had never been involved with literature that was quite so deep. In a lot of our discussions he would ask what did *we* think about it?"

Others, not in his class, found Chuck by accident or word of mouth. "I had a class right after one of his classes in the same classroom," said Cathy Hoff, daughter of two journalists. "He had a portion of the blackboard that said 'Do not erase' where he would write quotations. I thought that was a wonderful idea. And he was willing to talk about them with me even though I was not one of his regular students. Sometimes I would sneak in and write my own quotations up there. He liked that. And maybe the next time we would talk about the quotation. He was someone who wanted to talk about ideas, to share an intellectual conversation with students. I wish I had been in a class of his."

Bob Deppe, an IU kid and budding poet, was naturally drawn to Chuck and became a close friend, though never his student. "He was somebody you'd walk past his room and there would be all sorts of laughter going on. Music. Other students talked about him. I would sometimes stop by the room and talk a little bit with him. He was someone you wanted to know, somebody you're interested in."

Not only east-side kids were drawn to Chuck. Pruett, too, was intrigued by the quotations on the board and the discussions they sparked which she overheard with longing. She was in the English class of a matronly teacher where "we were tracing the outlines of our fingers to make turkeys. I talked to Chuck and he invited me to come speak to his class about a poem I wrote. I think he was throwing the dog a bone since I could not get a transfer."

As the year wore on a peer group of students steadily formed around "Mr. Walls" (some preferred "Chuckie" behind his back). The 1967 *Gothic* yearbook carries a photo taken in his classroom. Chuck is standing by a student's desk in his customary dark suit and narrow tie, his silky auburn hair swept across his forehead in a mild Beatles cut, sideburns above the ear. He's holding a copy of *Lord of the Flies* in one hand and exchanging smiles with Higgins, looking up from her copy of *Cuckoo's Nest*. He appears serene and untroubled.

Chuck Walls with student Kathy Higgins [*Gothic*, 1967]

It's the portrait of a young man happily engaged in his great passion, the art of pedagogy.

Behind Chuck on the wall is a bulletin board covered with clippings and photos reflecting his interest in music, politics and journalism: The front page of *The Indianapolis Star* on November 6, 1966, with the headline, "DRAFT CUT NEAR, LBJ TOLD." Images of the Righteous Brothers, Simon and Garfunkel on the album cover of *Parsley, Sage, Rosemary and Thyme,* and lists of the "HOT 100" and "TOP LP's." "Last Train to Clarksville" (The Monkees) topped the charts that week.

An Associated Press story under the LBJ headline reports, "Secretary of Defense Robert McNamara told President Johnson yesterday that fewer Americans will be sent to Viet Nam next year, and draft calls may be cut in half. McNamara bases his optimistic report on a military situation he said has been stabilized and dramatically improved."

Events over the next year would reveal both halcyon snapshots—Chuck at peace with himself and his place in the world; the U.S. on a path to certain victory in Vietnam—to have been mirages obscuring the misery and catastrophe to come.

Mahler, a more clear-eyed realist, saw "the level of animus from the establishment teachers and the administration toward someone who was so clearly outside the standards and norms" and feared for Chuck. "I remember feeling he seemed so vulnerable to a brutal system," he said. "I couldn't help but feel that the system was going to crush him."

Daydream Believers

Greg Dawson, Author's Note:

> In the summer of 1967, I commandeered my father's
> Oldsmobile and headed off with three BHS buddies to see
> the already-mythic Haight-Ashbury district in the flesh. Rid-
> ing shotgun in front with me was Bob Deppe, nascent poet;
> in back seat, Dan Sherman, future Bloomington city attor-
> ney, and Chris Hodenfield, my fellow cub reporter at the
> *Herald-Telephone*, headed for a career at *Rolling Stone*.

Hurtling west through rural Indiana on blue highways to meet up with
I-70 outside Terre Haute, windows rolled down, radio cranked up, we
were giddy, sick with excitement and new freedom, as if we were about
to leave Earth orbit. Reality bit hard when we burned up the engine in
Kansas. We spent three scorching days in a small town with yellow water
in the public pool while waiting for repairs, with no reefer to blot out the
fact that, Dammit, Toto, we're *still* in Kansas.

In San Francisco we slept on a misty hill above the city lights, mixed with
hippies in Golden Gate Park and freaks on Haight Street, saw Buffalo
Springfield and many colors at Fillmore West, and scored some seedy
weed. "We looked at that bag like it was a sackful of magic out of the Ara-
bian Nights," Chris recalls. We took it back to our seedy motel and
smoked it in a corncob pipe. No one got high that night but everyone's
paradigm got shifted.

Haight-Ashbury or bust. Clockwise from top left: Bob Deppe, Chris Hodenfield, Greg Dawson, Dan Sherman [*Gothic* photos from 1967 and 1968]

It turned out there was a lot of that going around that summer. Some-where a cosmic switch was thrown, a dog whistle blown, and 1967 became the coming out party for drugs in Bloomington.

"Before we went to San Francisco, I knew that some people smoked mar-ijuana and did drugs in town, but I couldn't have named anyone practi-cally," said Bob. "That was a whole different world. My friends didn't smoke pot. After I came back, almost everybody I knew smoked pot. I didn't see as much of other friends who didn't smoke. It was a whole dif-ferent culture I had been accepted into, or had chosen."

At an Army Surplus store in San Francisco, I picked up an oversized olive-green jungle fatigue jacket like the ones worn by G.I.s in Vietnam. It had deep pockets ideal for carrying plastic baggies of weed, pipes, foil and papers in and out of the house without raising the suspicion of parents. It was the unofficial uniform of a new army of potheads and dabblers.

Wally Brazy, one of Chuck's first sex partners when he student taught at BHS, spent his junior year studying in Spain. He left Bloomington in August 1966 and returned in the summer of '67 to a whole different culture.

"It didn't even look like the same university. It was just shocking. I can literally say that before I left, there was one student in one of my Span-ish classes who was considered an oddball because he didn't have a hair-cut and wore sandals. That was really radical. I came back and the hippies had arrived, and drugs. It was like Janis Joplin and her whole crew had been parachuted in. Everyone looked different and the music was different. People were sitting around in the grass, maybe they were stoned. Something had just exploded."

Not that Bloomington had been a drug-free zone before '67. There was certainly weed on the IU campus in 1963 when Dillingham was arrested. As pot began to spread off campus a logical destination was nearby Uni-versity High School. Soon the grass would be greener at BHS, too.

"In '66 weed was pretty much confined to U-School, but in early '67 it had hit BHS," said Dave Taggart, an early frequent flyer at BHS. "The first time I remember actually smoking it was maybe April, and it spread like wildfire. By the summer, drugs were all over the place."

If you were in the right place at the right time and knew the right people, the weed found you. "A friend said, 'Try this marijuana.' That's how I became a member of the counterculture," said Jon Pratter, a BHS student. "We had a group. It was sort of like a wave, everybody decided at the same time we wanted to engage in it."

Bogarting joints was a sacrilege. "Everyone shared pot with each other. If you had pot it would be shared" was how another BHS student, Nora Leill, explained the prevailing ethic in those first heady days of communal discovery.

Taggart said "most of the weed was coming from off-campus students, from traditional urban criminal centers like Indianapolis, Chicago and New York. There was a black guy, 'Box,' on west 6th or 7th who would sell nickels [$5 bags] to anybody who knocked on his door. His phrase was, 'later man.' People were going up to Nappanee [northern Indiana] and harvesting almost worthless, feral WW2-era hemp.

"There was a well-known dude who got his start delivering pizza and asking the customers if they wanted weed. He was bringing it in from California I believe. Some dorm kids from IU went down to Texas and came back with bushels of peyote, very foul shit. Bloomington was in the process of going from a retail to a wholesale market and different kinds of dope were suddenly all over the place. Some of my friends had started shooting meth, which brought matters quickly to a head for them.

"Acid was coming from California, by mail from the Brotherhood of Eternal Love. I have on my wall a price list a friend sent me from San Francisco in the summer of '67. I imported acid a couple of times. One thing I wish I'd saved was the hollowed out book—*Hell's Angels*, Hunter Thompson—I got a shipment of acid in once. In the summer of '67 getting a few tabs from San Francisco was a big deal. By the spring of '68 mass quantities of different kinds of acid as well as psilocibyn, meth and hash were available on Kirkwood."

Brazy, an abstainer, surveyed a scene where "a lot of strange things happened. People disappeared, they went hitchhiking, they came back and you saw they had obviously done a lot of drugs, and were dancing with parking meters, and had lost some of their teeth and half of their memory."

Up close, Bloomington didn't look like a major transit point for drugs, a mid-sized town in southern Indiana hemmed in by two-lane roads. But pull back for an atlas view and it's apparent why it was ideally situated to blossom as a drug mecca. Interstates crisscrossed the state. I-65 became a Silk Road for the drug trade, running from Chicago to the Gulf where shrimp boats of Colombian pot arrived for shipment north.

Steve Higgs grew up in a working-class neighborhood on the east side of Indianapolis. He was drawn to mecca by the prospect of Babylonian pleasures of body and mind.

"I came from an anti-intellectual, working-class background. I wanted to go to Purdue. Then politics came along, and IU was where the politics were, where the counterculture was, where the protests were. I found a copy of *The Spectator* [underground paper] that had a full-page picture of a naked girl from behind walking up the steps of the Indiana Memorial Union. I wanted to be there."

Higgs enrolled at IU in the late '60s and spent a decade as a low-level dealer. He was busted once, on a minor possession charge. He pled guilty, was given probation, and went back to dealing.

"You can talk Madison and Ann Arbor and these other places, but there aren't many places in the United States where you have the demographics of Bloomington, where half to two-thirds of the community has some level of college education," Higgs said. "Then you had this mix of southern libertarian personalities: 'I don't care what you do as long as you leave me alone.' That combination of attitude and demographics plus location: within 60 miles of Indianapolis, two hours from Louisville. But what made the place really tick was the Region [Northwest Indiana] connection. All the people I was involved with were from the Region. That's who was buying off the boats. Big-time dealers three or four hours outside Chicago.

"I was one person away from the people who were buying marijuana directly from Colombia. There were people in Bloomington buying boatloads of marijuana. In the early days they got it from the southwest. All of a sudden it went from $15 bags of Mexican to $30 bags of Colombian. People were driving past each other on highway 45 with truckloads of marijuana who didn't even know each other.

"Millions and millions of dollars passed through town, trickled down to the economy. I heard of right-wing Republicans who profited in those days. Up and down Kirkwood, drug money was all over the place."

It was pumped into boutiques, head shops, import stores, sandwich shops, pool parlors. The expanding pot pie sustained a small army of nickel-dime doorstep dealers like "Box" and "Big Barb" and "Chris Sunshine" and "New York Andy" as well as serious import-export entrepreneurs dealing in 50-pound bales stacked to the ceiling in safe houses around town.

"The underground economy supported thousands of guys like me through direct and indirect cash flow. Full and part-time dealers at all levels: cooks, store clerks, servers," Higgs said. "Money trickled down to restaurants and car dealerships. I remember walking into an audio store and walking out with an entire stereo system because I had the money in my pocket."

Higgs didn't get rich. "I had no desire to become Johnny Depp [in the movie *Blow*] because there was a downside that went along with those guys. I saw their decline and I saw their falls." But he did know some who got filthy with lucre and flaunted it. There was the player who asked Higgs for a ride one day to a Bloomington car dealership.

"I picked him up and drove him down to Royal Chevrolet and he drove out with a 2000 40 Z. It was the first model they made, emerald green. It was the most ostentatious thing you've ever seen. Hair down to his shoulders, got his turquoise jewelry, his dope-dealer outfit to the hilt. He pays cash, hops in the car and drives back to his house out in the country."

Higgs stayed in Bloomington and made sure he wouldn't get rich, going to work as a reporter for the *Herald-Telephone*. Dan "Carp" Combs took a similar vow of relative poverty, teaching history at BHS and serving as a township trustee, repeatedly re-elected by voters he says know all about his first job and just don't care.

Dave Taggart

Carp Combs

[*Gothic* 1968] and Courtesy of Carp Combs circa 1969

In the '60s, Combs was a kid from the boonies who came to town looking for a part-time job and ended up "a local franchisee" within the vast Bloomington drug network. One of his jobs was to drive pot-laden cars to places like Fort Wayne, park them on the street in front of designated houses, and walk away. Then he would be picked up and returned home.

That was a few years down the road. It took a while for the rural stripling to be corrupted, to buckle to temptations dangled by his elders, IU students he worked with in the "dish room" at the Union. Combs grew up in Harrodsburg, a U-turn in the road 10 miles south of Bloomington, and went to high school in Smithville, another hamlet. Chances of finding a job at home were slim to none.

"So we went to the Union Building for jobs, and there was this hierarchy. The stonies, the hick kids, we worked in the dish rooms. Huge mechanized dish rooms. Very dirty, very wet, really kind of dangerous work. That was where the Harrodsburg and Smithville kids went. The University High and Bloomington High kids worked in catering, the clean jobs, serving banquets in Alumni Hall, the Solarium, the Federal and Georgian rooms. We barely interacted with them even though they would be bringing these huge trays and carts of stuff for us to wash.

"Unlucky IU students needing a work-study job got stuck with us. That was my first exposure to pot. I remember them giving it to me. You would get little wooden match boxes. A match box was called a nickel, five bucks, or half an ounce. It was really horrible pot, seeds and stuff. It was a couple years before I took my first hit because I was raised on *Reefer Madness* in Smithville. They showed us propaganda. In health class they would bring in the 16 mm projector and show us military films, old newsreels. It was a pretty horrifying thought to smoke marijuana. But after being around the IU kids for a couple years, and nobody overdosed and nobody died, no one turned into a raving lunatic, I was desensitized to the horror stories."

If Bloomington was a mecca for hinterland Hoosiers, Dunn Meadow behind the Union was Max Yasgur's farm in miniature, a grassy expanse wider than an aircraft carrier, longer than three football fields, encircled by maples and oaks that blazed in the autumn, bisected by a clear-running brook misnomered the Jordan River. All manner of Woodstockian activity played out there in the '60s, with less mud and nudity and better sanitation.

"In the '60s there was always some celebration going on in the meadow," Combs said. "You didn't need permits from IU back then. If you wanted to have a concert, you just went down there and had a concert. In the afternoon and evenings, going up those steps, limestone ledges on either side, there would be almost stereotypical hippies—leather hats, finger cymbals and all sorts of stuff—and when you walked by they were whispering, 'acid, acid, acid, mescaline, mescaline, mescaline, reefer, reefer.' Larry Bizarri was IU's narc. Everyone knew him. He'd come through the meadow wearing disguises, and when he'd go up the steps the dealers would go, 'Hi, Larry!' just to bug him.

"I remember the first Afghanistan black hash I ever smoked was in Dunn Meadow. I was with my brother, who later died from drug-induced psychosis. We climbed up one of those big Sycamore trees by the Jordan River, sitting on a limb, and he said, 'Here' and handed me a pipe. It makes you cough and expands in your lungs, and all of a sudden I'm higher than I've been smoking anything. I kind of froze in the tree. He finally said, 'I'm gettin' down.' He gets down and says, 'Hey, watch my brother up there. He's high and can't get out of the tree.' There was a small group of hippies under the tree doing a circular dance, chanting, trying to chant me down. After that I was pretty much accepted in the Dunn Meadow scene."

It's not clear when Chuck first dipped his toe in the emerging drug culture, and who turned him on. It could have been Jim Sutton, Class of '68, whose father, Joe, was named IU president that year and had a brief, tumultuous tenure, resigning in 1970 after the death of his wife from cancer. Jim died at 46 of myriad addictions.

"Jimmy and Chuck were pretty close and they were hanging out and smoking dope and doing a lot of that stuff," said his younger brother Geoff Sutton. "Jimmy was pretty inspired by him. They went to England together. I can't speak exactly to Chuck's involvement in it, but Jimmy brought back a bunch of clinical LSD from Oxford. I did my first LSD trip on that acid."

Geoff supplied a circle of buddies and for a while they planned their weekends around tripping and listening to music in the basements of their parents' homes. Liell, two years behind Jimmy at BHS, also tripped for the first time on Jimmy's import. "Nobody knew what a 'hit' was so I took an eyedropper full. I was like 14. Last thing I remember I was hanging onto a pole in an apartment praying that it would be over soon."

Given his generous impulse to serve as a hallucinogenic Johnny Appleseed, it's easy to imagine Jimmy was the one to offer Chuck his first joint, and perhaps a hit from the brown bottle. If it wasn't Jimmy, Taggart is a good candidate and can attest to it. He had Chuck for English his junior year.

"I was pretty evangelical about weed and acid in those days," Taggart said. "I gave Walls some weed and got high with him, either in fall '67 or early '68. A street runaway 'Mr. New York' and I rode around with Walls in his blue Camaro smoking one night and it stalled out in the boonies. We went to the nearest house and this weird hillbilly took us into town. I don't remember getting high with Walls except that one time, but I'm pretty sure I sold him nickels or dimes on more than one occasion."

As the tide of drugs rose inexorably around them, school officials remained as numbly oblivious as the proverbial frog in a pot of cold water slowly coming to a boil that will cook him. There were, here and there, subtle signs for those who could discern them.

An edition of *The Optimist* early in the 67-68 school year included this entry from the popular "Did you notice?" column: "Did you notice...Mr. Jones and Mr. Milne chasing all the kids out of their cars at lunch?" It might have been Geoff Sutton and his buddies, and an army of others. They were not searching their cars for homework notes. "We'd go out at lunch and everybody would get stoned then go back to class," Sutton said.

Bill Sturbaum had a student in his social studies class who "would come back from lunch and put his head on his desk. I never let kids put their heads on their desks. I would go to him and say, 'You look sick. Let's go to see the nurse.' It was obvious he'd been smoking pot during the lunch hour."

Medlyn, the guidance counselor for sophomores and juniors at BHS, was among the first to sense the incoming tide. The number of students who came to her office to talk about drugs increased "exponentially" in '66 and '67. Drug issues were familiar to Medlyn, who had worked as a psychiatric social worker.

"There was a kid who smoked too much, and he came to my office and he was hallucinating. I knew when a kid was hallucinating. He'd sit there and look at the wall and start to giggle. And I said to him, the wall is moving isn't it? I felt responsible for him. I couldn't just let him go. I got a nurse to call the doctor in. He had no exposure to drugs. So he said to this kid, 'What did you eat yesterday?' The kid started to giggle at the top of his voice and I said, 'The doctor is asking you silly questions, isn't he?'

"For a while they referred to me as a drug counselor, which I didn't like because I neglected other kids for the kids who were on drugs. I knew they came from IU families and college was in their future. About the only thing I had going with them was a scare tactic. 'If you smoke grass it's going to fry your brain, and you're college material.' That made sense to some of them.

"The kids from the country thought that smoking grass was a very effete sort of thing. Just pansy stuff. What you really want to get is your beer and your booze. Eventually the country kids, the 'old Bloomington' kids who never stepped on [IU] campus, started using it too. When I tried to use the same scare tactic on them it didn't seem to work.

"I told the administration that we had a problem. They said I would have to report it, that I also had to report pregnancies. I said, no, if they tell me confidentially, I won't tell you. I told [principal] Joe Cull, I'm not going to report anybody who's pregnant because they need to go to school more than anybody. And as far as the drug use is concerned, be aware that it's going on, but I'm not going to report an individual who's using it. And he accepted that, which surprised me."

About the same time, David Johnson, pastor of the Unitarian Universalist Church, was trying to alert school officials to the growing presence of drugs. Johnson participated in a clergy consultation service, which counseled young men about the draft among other issues, and his child attended a co-op nursery school. His multifaceted role in the community gave him an unusually keen radar.

"I picked up a lot of information I would not otherwise have known," Johnson said. "I became aware there were drugs in the high schools. And it was a little while later I realized they had gotten down to middle school. We had a very active and intelligent congregation, including several teachers, so they were very much aware. It was through parents that I first heard things and decided to pursue them."

His entreaties to high school officials were so blithely and thoroughly dismissed that he gave up.

"I didn't talk to administrators at the junior high level because I had talked to so many at the high school level. It was at some public meeting that I said, 'I'm hearing that it's in the junior high,' and that's when I got this furious response. I wish I could remember who I talked to in the school system, but I do remember the furious response. It was an absolute turndown of the whole question. They said, 'You don't know. You don't understand. There is nothing here.'"

One Toke Over the Line

"*D*id you notice...Mr. Walls' orange and blue-striped shirt with the purple paisley tie?"

The Optimist noticed. Everyone noticed. Chuck Walls went to England a poster boy for Sears Roebuck and came back a character in a Peter Max poster. Gone were the monochrome wardrobe and careful coif of the first-year teacher. He stood transformed before his students the first day of class in September, 1967.

"He was very much the Beatles. The Beatles in their funky time, before they got way out there and were into India and gurus," said Al King, a sophomore that fall. "He had on a yellow bow tie, one you had to tie yourself. I'd never see one before, just clip-ons. He was kind of the Yellow Submarine Beatle. He even had the hair. It was a little bit curly, and he was sort of trying to manage this long moppy mess before they had learned how to cut it."

As a secret gay traveler in the straight and narrow culture of Bloomington High School, King was better able to view Chuck's makeover with curiosity and a degree of empathy as a fellow outlier. But to the great majority of students in the mainstream, the new Chuck was an exotic.

"The moment I laid eyes on him it wasn't something I was expecting to see," said Mark Rieger , a doctor's son and member of the JV football team. "The way he dressed and his crazy hair, his friendly smile and his animation. I don't think there was anyone who didn't take note of the fact that Mr. Walls was quite different from anything we had experienced before."

Word had gotten around in Chuck's first year about his unorthodox techniques. What Rieger and King observed at the outset of Chuck's second year was mostly not about technique but something more fundamental and perilous: a teacher who had switched allegiance to the brotherhood of students while maintaining his role as teacher.

It was a charade bound to collapse of its own contradictions. The six weeks in England and France when he sometimes crossed over from chaperone to ring leader of extracurricular adventures had emboldened Chuck in breaching the wall that preserves a degree of separation and formality between student and teacher. He never wanted to be "Mr. Chips."

"Of course we called him Mr. Walls to his face, but to each other we used to call him Chuck Walls instead of Charles Walls," said Anne Schmitz. "And I used to think it was strange that we knew his name was Chuck because most of our teachers, we didn't know what their name was."

It was not strange. It was Chuck's desire, communicated both subliminally and overtly. Once in a note to a student he wrote: "You may NOT call me Charles! It must be...Chuck."

The students he fraternized with and led on escapades in England would become members of the peer group he never found among fellow teachers, the college frat he never had. The alienation Chuck felt from day one at BHS deepened over the summer and blossomed into full-blown separation by the start of the new school year.

"I remember the way his clothing and style changed during the time we were in England, how the other teachers treated him with disdain both on the trip and at home," said Pruett, who witnessed the cold rage of co-chaperone Virginia Elkin the day Chuck overslept and kept the bus waiting.

For Elkin the tardiness was symptomatic of everything she did not like about this young man, which was everything. His easy rapport with students had to be galling to her. His consorting with them, his disrespect for the sacred wall, was abhorrent to Elkin. And she was keeping score.

"I heard about his chumming around with students from Ginny Elkin," said colleague Donnadee Blair. "You have to remember that Chuck had already moved his loyalty to students and not faculty. I thought he was foolish and told him what a risk he was taking on losing his job. But he had pretty much stopped talking to me by then.

"It was a time of abandonment for free spirits, of which the BHS administration was *not*. He knew Ginny Elkin would tattle on him to John Jones and I think he just denied it and threw it all to the wind. That was how I read Chuck when he returned from London."

He hit the ground running, riskily, starting with his stewardship of *The Optimist*. Though Chuck spent his first year as editorial advisor, his name was not on the masthead and it was difficult to find his fingerprints on the content. He deferred to Bill Gosser, the venerable supervisor who put out a school paper that slavishly mirrored its name. Now that Chuck was listed as Editorial Advisor, and Gosser just the production advisor, deference gave way to daring.

EDITORIAL STAFF . . . Front row: Yvette Hall, Nancy Barr, Veronica Sebeock, Editor-in-Chief Debbie Richardson, Peggy Pruett, Helen Smith, Kim Schmalz. Second row: Patty Miller, Kathy Snedegar, Patricia Haeberle, John White, Gary Denewett, Sally Sibbitt, Mary Ann Mathews, Geoff Grodner, Mary Ann Sturdevant, Larry Vermeulen. Third row: Jim Holmes, Harold Christy, Sara Zylman, Gail Middleton, Nancy Chapman, Chris Simpson, Liz Flaten, Betsy Barr, Kathy Westie.

Optimist staff, 1967-68 [*Gothic*, 1968]

In August, Nancy Barr, a senior who worked on *The Optimist* the previous year, was invited to a pre-school meeting of student editors at Chuck's apartment, which he shared with Ray Maudlin, a former IU classmate who was teaching at Spencer High School while getting his master's. Barr, slated as news editor for the upcoming year, said the only other invitees were Debbie Richardson (editor in chief) and Veronica Sebeok (opinion editor).

"My parents were adamant that it was improper and that I wouldn't be going," Barr said. "Debbie Richardson and I talked. Her parents felt the same way. They agreed we could go together in the same car and leave together. We were to leave if there was any impropriety.

"I drove to Mr. Walls' apartment near the Big Wheel [restaurant] on Cascades Park Road. Veronica Sebeok answered the door. Mr. Walls was on the sofa. Veronica proceeded to play hostess, offering us sodas and snacks. She was barefoot, casually dressed and very comfortable and familiar with his apartment.

"I knew that didn't seem right but wouldn't have known what to think beyond that. The apartment was not well lit and the curtains were closed. I was anxious to get out of there. The meeting was short and we did get out quickly. I don't remember what Debbie and I said but remember we both were kind of stunned. I did know I would never go there again."

Richardson is certain that she never visited Chuck's apartment. "My parents would have never allowed me to go under any circumstances. If Nancy recalls going, it was *not* with me." Double-checking her memory, Barr said, "No, it was Debbie."

Sebeok said, "I remember neither the creepy evening, nor most of the named players except Nancy Barr. I would not have felt uncomfortable at Chuck's apartment. My comfort was in the security that there would be no sexual threat whatever from Chuck. Oh God, what a life poor Chuck had to lead. Of course he had to keep the curtains closed."

His door, however, remained open. Chuck's apartment became a sort of salon for friends and favored students who enjoyed getting high on weed and words. "Many students would go there," said a girl in Chuck's inner circle. "We did get high. Listened to The Doors a lot. And just talked. You know how it is when you're that age. Everything is so important, you've discovered it for the first time. It was intellectually stimulating. We weren't enticed there because he was going to give us drugs. It wasn't like, 'Come over. I'm going to get you high.' We could have gone anywhere to get high."

He doesn't remember why or exactly when, but Geoff Grodner found his way to Chuck's apartment one night. "I think it was the first time I ever smoked dope. I don't know if he gave it to me, but it was there." That fall Chuck recruited Grodner to work on *The Optimist.*

Kellar knew Chuck from the trip to England "when I lost my innocence," but waited till she got back to start doing drugs.

"I visited his apartment, he visited our house when my parents weren't there. There were long phone calls. A group of us would meet him in out-of-the-way places so people wouldn't know, sometimes at night. A cemetery, not far from Bob's [Deppe] house, a grade school on that side of town. I don't really remember but I imagine we did smoke dope."

Chuck's behavior went from risky to reckless. He began showing up at student parties where weed was present. Deppe remembered a party at Kellar's home. "We were smoking pot, and at a certain point in the party Chuck showed up. In a poem, I have him dressed in a Sherlock Holmes outfit, but I think that's fantasy. He joined us, we all had a good time. He smoked too."

Andy Mahler valued Chuck as a teacher but worried that in his naiveté he was sleepwalking toward a cliff. He was startled to see Chuck at another house party. "I thought it was not a great idea for a teacher to come to a party where dope was being smoked. I can't remember who asked me or how it came up, but at some point, in a formal capacity, I was asked if Chuck had been there and I said no. I was covering for him."

Inside the walls of BHS, Chuck began lighting little fires of rebellion among friends. Many were self-professed misfits and outsiders allergic to "school spirit" in any form especially pep rallies before school football and basketball games. One time he opened up *The Optimist* darkroom for students who wanted to escape a required pep rally.

"He invited students in who wanted to discuss books that had been banned or frowned on by the English department," Deppe said. "He was specifically interested in *Cuckoo's Nest*. He suggested we look for parallels between Virginia Elkin and Nurse Ratched."

Chuck and Deppe were on separate collision courses with Elkin. Both were playing rebellious psychiatric hospital patient Randall Patrick McMurphy to Elkin's despotic Nurse Ratched in the view of one compatriot in the secret reading group.

"We saw in that institution everything that was going on in the institution of the school. We all saw it as a complete mirror. We were all aware of having a persecution complex, but with good reason."

As a junior Deppe took creative writing from Elkin. All was sweetness and light. "It was the only time in my life I was a teacher's pet. I wrote sappy love poems and she ate it up. Then senior year everything changed. Chuck's comparing Virginia Elkin to Nurse Ratched helped me feel she wasn't somebody I should take seriously, and it was okay to push the envelope. I was writing imitation Camus and Sartre plays. All the characters had French names, depressing ideas, and talked suicide. Virginia Elkin thought they disturbed the other kids. The swear words I thought were necessary for great art were not okay with her. She eventually kicked me out of the class."

It didn't end there. Nurse Elkin also kicked Deppe out of her senior English class despite his passing grades. "She gave me an 'F' and said my attitude was poor. And she refused to take me back for the spring semester." School officials let Deppe take courses at IU and transfer the credits he needed to graduate. (Deppe's career path would include time as a psychiatric nurse which informed much of the writing in his acclaimed career as teacher, poet and author.)

While his subterfuges with the darkroom and Elkin played out in the shadows, known only to a few, Chuck's attempted makeover of *The Optimist* into something more than a bulletin board for pablum became an ongoing melodrama drawing the attention and involvement of many.

"The first week of school I remember trying to get into Mr. Walls' room through the door between his and Mr. Gosser's room," said Nancy Barr. "It was impossible. A group of kids was always blocking the door. It seemed as if only that group was allowed in his room, everyone else was not permitted. Being very impatient and always on task, it didn't take long for me to turn only to Mr. Gosser for whatever I needed."

Even before the awkward encounter at Chuck's apartment, Barr was dispirited by the change of leadership. "I was not happy that Mr. Walls was put in charge of *The Optimist*. Mr. Gosser was one of my favorite teachers. I learned much from him."

Barr saw nothing in Chuck's performance to allay her misgivings—it looked like a train wreck to her—and once again they parted under awkward circumstances.

"Stories weren't being assigned, few were being written or turned in by deadline. It was a very lean year with papers coming out late and a few times not at all. Mr. Walls started coming in the paste-up room where I stayed after school trying to make each issue happen. He would touch my shoulder or arm, standing so close I could feel his breath as he commented on the layout.

"I was very uncomfortable. After a few times, I only stayed as long as Mr. Gosser was there. I avoided Mr. Walls, leaving the room if he entered, and I don't think I ever said another word to him. I got an 'A' in his class, which I did earn but was surprised since there was no student/teacher exchange."

Debbie Richardson, from her chair as editor-in-chief, seemed to be watching a different movie.

"I must give credit to Chuck that we even had a paper. I was so frustrated by lack of support from Gosser that I welcomed any suggestions or improvements from Chuck. I wrote an article that was slightly critical of teachers, and I remember going to [principal] John Jones' office and being 'urged' to rewrite it. When I got back to the classroom, Gosser just said kill it. He didn't want any problems with his supervisor, even though he had job security.

"I don't know if Chuck fought the administration on this, but my articles and editorials ran without any more of the paper's staff being called down to the office. I knew I wasn't going to be employed as a journalist, but I still wanted to be proud of what I did and welcomed any changes to stop the paper from being a joke. I admired Chuck's courage in standing up for changes and for the writers. I'm sure he was told he had to toe the line or face non-renewal of his contract."

Despite his masthead title as editorial advisor, Chuck was hamstrung by the fact that Gosser retained a veto he could exercise at any time. Even so, under Chuck's guidance *The Optimist* became something it had never been—a forum for politics, music, movies, literature, poetry, short stories, even haiku. It still reported the eternal staples of high school such as homecoming queens, ballgames, prom prep, academic honors and staff changes, and continued fluffy features like "Did you Notice?"

"Did you notice Karl Sturbaum's fluorescent green socks...Pam Kinser doing the 'Funky Broadway' in the cafeteria at lunch hour...Andy Mahler lying on the floor of *The Optimist* room...Mr. Walls and Jim Sutton in their mod clothes from England?"

But now the fluff was balanced by substance and real journalism. There were reviews of movies (*A Man for All Seasons*), books (*The Great Gatsby*), and albums from the Beatles, Stones, Jimi Hendrix, Donovan, Vanilla Fudge, and Tim Buckley. In October '67, a full page was devoted to opposing views of the war, "The Left and Right of Vietnam." There were stories about students involved in the McCarthy and Kennedy campaigns, and a senior, Kevin Craig, who told a community forum on civil liberties, "Our education teaches us to live under authoritarian controls. If this is the goal of the school, it's doing a good job."

Essays poked sacred cows of conventional wisdom and morality. In "Affluence—the Dehumanizing Influence," Mahler wrote, "We are poor where it really counts, in the mind," and wondered if his generation would "cast off the yoke of wealth-worship so predominant in this country. Will we find ourselves and beauty, not in physical things but true beauty, the beauty of the mind?"

Under the headline, "Puritanism, Plague of Society?," Trix Whitehall wrote: "Puritanism is the fear that someone will be not only happy, but a tinge different from his staid fellow human being. It seems that spontaneity and idiosyncrasy are subversive to everything the nice, quiet, ridiculous middle class stands for."

Kellar contributed a macabre short story about a young woman visiting a cemetery with her husband to choose the perfect resting place for their unborn child. It was all a bit much for staid sensibilities of the ridiculous middle class.

"I remember my mom seeing an issue of *The Optimist* when Chuck was in charge," King said. "I laid my books on the dining room table and she picked it up to read. She said, 'Why is this stuff in a high school newspaper?'"

No doubt administrators were thinking the same thing. The train wreck was starting to look like a runaway train of free expression. They drew the line at an article urging students to cut class and protest a speech at IU by Secretary of State Dean Rusk, there to defend U.S. policy in Vietnam where the U.S. death count was nearly 20,000 and rising. He spoke the day after Bloomington police arrested 35 IU students who staged a sit-in at the business school where Dow Chemical, maker of napalm, was conducting job interviews. Some of the students forcibly removed from the scene were beaten and bloodied by police.

The piece was written by two students not on *The Optimist* staff: Deppe and Kent Harvey, a brilliant malcontent and son of the dean of IU's law school. Someone alerted higher-ups and the boys were summoned to the office of assistant principal Bill Milne, widely regarded as Jones' enforcer.

"We were told that our editorial wouldn't be allowed in *The Optimist*," Deppe recalled. "We said, but it's a student newspaper, we are students, this is our voice, this is what we think. And we were told, honest to God, 'You're not here in high school to learn to think, you are here to learn a body of facts. When you go to university you'll be able to apply those facts, and there you will learn how to think.'

"And I said, 'Please repeat that. Tell me we are not here in high school to learn to think.' Affirmed. Chuck Walls was the antithesis of that. Chuck was urging us all to think."

And to speak and to write in exercise of the First Amendment, part of the "body of facts" that BHS students were there to learn (while not learning to think). Milne had no patience for the invoking of Constitutional rights.

Brandishing a paddle for emphasis, he informed one parent, "This is what keeps order here, not the Constitution."

Authority Always Wins

*I*n the fall of 1967 the winds of change and liberation sweeping across America had not yet penetrated the limestone walls of Bloomington High School where iron rule maintained an environment more reminiscent of East Germany than Haight-Ashbury.

"So much was changing in the larger national community, but not at BHS," said *Optimist* editor Richardson. "Faculty, administrators, and community leaders did not welcome questions or suggestions from students or anyone that encouraged students to think outside the box."

"Students were very compliant," said counselor Ida Medlyn. "Ninety-nine point nine percent of the time they did what they were told to do."

Administrators continued to monitor hair length and hem lines. The first day of school 10 boys with longish hair were not allowed to enroll—sent home with instructions to return with neater looks. Several girls were banished and told to come back in longer skirts. The era's prevailing benchmark for skirt length: when kneeling, the hem should touch the floor.

"We believe there is a relationship between dress and conduct," said assistant Milne. "Our students want to do what is right. They're just waiting for someone to tell them what is expected of them."

Administrators claimed the right to search student lockers without notice, using a master key. Articles in the school newspaper opposing government policy were verboten. Leaving the campus to exercise free speech at political protests was strictly forbidden.

Deppe and Harvey, co-authors of the aborted *Optimist* article urging students to boycott class to protest Rusk's talk at IU, heeded their own call and were suspended for two days, as were some two dozen classmates. Another group of students who stayed in school but wore black armbands in solidarity also suffered the wrath of Milne.

"It was a black armband with a star of David and it said 'Peace.' We had on our very conservative clothing—pleated wool skirt, mohair sweater, knee-high socks and penny loafers. We got suspended from school for the day just for wearing an armband," said a junior girl.

On another occasion, students wore armbands to protest the presence of the Crane Naval Ammunition Depot 45 miles southwest of Bloomington which produced munitions used in Vietnam.

"Milne said if we were going to wear armbands to protest Crane then we had to wear armbands every day," said Kathy May, whose father started the religious studies department at IU. "And I said to him, 'You mean like a yellow star?'"

Coach Goss, who brooked no dissent from his athletes, regarded the protests as a sort of contagious virus. "I wondered if we would ever survive it. I remember the rallies in Dunn Meadow. We had kids wanting to go to them and that was kind of 'no.' That was off limits, you didn't go."

Direct opposition to the war in *The Optimist* was out of the question. But in a pre-Thanksgiving editorial, Richardson bravely, if tortuously, defended the students' right to protest by conflating the Rusk and Dow protests and invoking the Pilgrims as the "the original dissenters."

"The recent demonstrations at IU and the turmoil surrounding the wearing of armbands at BHS are instances of today's dissension," she wrote. "But while everyone applauds the Pilgrims for their courage in dissenting, the actions of those today are condemned."

It was left unsaid that like the phone calls in a slasher movie, condemnation of the dissident students was coming from inside the house. (Lucky for the Pilgrims that Milne was not on board the Mayflower.) "I was trying to support student rights to express opinions in a way that would allow the editorial to be printed," Richardson said.

There were isolated acts of civil disobedience and defiance of front office decrees. Girls like Kellar, who returned from England with Carnaby Street mini-skirts, learned to use the administrators' hem-line obsession for their own purposes.

"On days you had exams you wore them and walked by the principal's office right before the class you were having the test in," Kellar said. "You got sent home to change clothes, so you didn't have to take the test that day. I did that a couple times, and I'm sure others did it."

Besides a purple mini-skirt and two bottles of French champagne for her parents, Lucy Darby stepped off the plane in Indianapolis with an altered self-image forged by study at Oxford and random uncharted experiences, some with Chuck. "It was a very liberating time for me," Darby said. "I was not the same girl."

The trip had stiffened Darby's already sturdy spine and left her in no mood to bend to petty tyranny from above.

"I was asked to cut my hair when I made the varsity cheerleading squad. There were two of us who refused to cut our hair—me and Becky Blackwell. The cheerleading sponsor, she was old, she wanted us all to be the same. Our parents just said, 'Are you kidding me?' It got to be a real stink. The team voted to give us our letters even though we didn't cheer because we were basically forced out. It kind of changed my whole flavor of high school."

Darby's English teacher that fall was aware of her rebellion and had reason to sympathize. He, too, was refusing to cut his hair which had grown thicker over the summer, curling up in back, sideburns creeping well below the ear lobes. His appearance deviated radically from the shorn-sheep look favored by Jones and the others, except those who Bryl-creemed their short locks into shiny submission.

It was asking a lot for Chuck to cut his hair, said Blair. "In those days your hair represented you. I mean, look at the Beatles. I had real long hair. Chuck's hair was beautiful, kind of reddish blonde, and he let it grow to the point you couldn't see his eyebrows. You could just see his eyes. It was Chuck's 'crown of glory.' We joked about it because his dad was a minister."

The story in Chuck's eyes had changed. There is a group photo in the '68 *Gothic* taken in fall '67 of the students and chaperones who had traveled to Europe that summer. They are standing in three jumbled rows on steps outside the school. Chuck is in the middle of the last row, holding a folded copy of *The Times of London* at chest level. The buoyancy and boyishness of previous photos are gone. There is no light in his eyes. He has the blank stare of a hostage.

Oxford travelers, fall 1967 [*Gothic*, 1968]

Chuck's delinquent hair likely wouldn't have risen above the level of a speeding ticket if Jones hadn't seen it as emblematic of a general insubordination. And now there were rumors of sex and drugs coming to his attention. He or Milne, his hallway eyes and ears, may have heard it on the grapevine or directly from Elkin, who seeded the grapevine with gossip after returning from England.

When students reported in late August for the start of classes, "the rumor spread quickly that Mr. Walls had inappropriate, but consensual, physical contact with one or more of the young ladies on the England trip," said Mary Carmichael, a junior. The rumor was believable since "a good number of the female students at BHS had crushes on him because he was young and handsome," and only a few people had any inkling Chuck was gay.

Nancy Anderson, who was in Chuck's 10th grade English class, heard "the whispered allegation he was consorting with female students, but I always considered that to be part of a smear campaign on the part of the faculty or administration or both."

Chuck was young and dynamic but "an odd duck for the BHS faculty," Anderson said. "He started a literary magazine but the shop teacher in charge of printing it refused because there was a review of a book he objected to, *Catcher in the Rye,* I think. I wanted my mother to confront the administration but she refused and that was probably in keeping with the times."

Jones already was wary of Chuck from reports of his unorthodox classroom methods, but playing "I Am a Rock" was not a firing offense. The rumors he was hearing now about Chuck, if true, might be enough.

"I do know that something happened on that trip," Sturbaum said. "I don't know what it was. I sensed it. John Jones' daughter was on the trip. And when rumors started to go around, John was asked to investigate the situation and asked me to go in and observe the class."

Sturbaum saw nothing that would help Jones build a case against Chuck. "It was first-rate teaching. He had a lesson plan, he had class participation, there was just a good feeling in that classroom. I thought the kids respected him." Two history teachers, Don Beaver and Gus Burchfield, observed on another day with the same result.

"We went just because everybody was talking about him. It was controversy," Beaver said. "He was a *good* teacher. He was different. He had his class reading some book, don't ask me what it was, but it was considered sexy. There was a teacher who had a daughter in the class. He just blew his lid. Good Catholic boy and his daughter was reading this filth."

Mark Rieger, son of a urologist, admittedly "a straight arrow and a little bit naive," had Chuck for English that fall, his junior year.

"I remember bringing home a syllabus of what we were going to be reading and my dad got ahold of it. He saw titles he wasn't familiar with like *Animal Farm* and *Brave New World*. His main question was, 'Why aren't you reading really well-known authors?' The kind of books *he* likes, Michener and on down the line. Those guys were storytellers and I think Mr. Walls was interested in authors that provoked thought."

A couple of weeks later on a Saturday afternoon Rieger came home after hanging out with friends and was jolted out of his weekend reverie.

"I went out to the back, and there were my folks sitting on the porch with Chuck Walls. I was totally shocked. I thought, 'What is going on here? Am I in trouble, and what am I in trouble *for?* Chuck looks up, smiles, and waves. They're drinking. They've all got a glass in front of them. I didn't know what to think.

"It turned out that my dad had contacted Chuck and invited him over to have a chat about what we were learning. My dad was a voracious reader. He read everything he could get his hands on. I sat down with them for a while then got up and let them continue their conversation. As far as I know, they had a good time."

Dr. Rieger fetched a pile of books from his collection, classic titles, and the convivial conversation went on past happy hour. Speaking with elders on their terms was a milieu in which Chuck was comfortable and had always excelled, summoning the politesse of a minister's son. Rieger's parents were reassured, even charmed. His older sister, Corry, a senior, was not so sanguine. She was never in Chuck's class but had watched him and was uneasy.

"I had a class right across from where he had his class, and I would see him standing outside his door interacting with kids all the time, clustered around him. It really stood out that he was having conversations with them and wasn't hurrying back to his room to prepare for class or anything.

"It was real secretive, whatever the kids were talking to him about. There were allusions to drugs and stuff, but they were very guarded about what they would say. So I was kind of scared of him. There seemed to be a lack of boundaries. It wasn't really clear that he was the teacher and the students were the students."

Corry noticed that things had changed over the summer. More people were smoking dope, and she found herself drifting away from some friends.

"There was a feeling that your friends weren't your friends anymore, and it was related to Chuck Walls. Certain ones had kind of designated themselves as the really cool kids, you know, because they hung out with him. There was just this invisible wall."

Whether you ended up on Chuck's side of the wall with the cool kids depended partly on how you responded to his teaching.

"He was a really good teacher," said Schmitz. "But he was very critical and had a very narrow view of what he wanted from his students. He wanted us to question everything. I don't think he was very tolerant of people who didn't question. If you were analytical you were going to be okay in his class, though he was probably going to set you to a different standard you didn't think was appropriate. I think he had definite favorites."

Linda Aynes was not among them. She relished the assignments to write about Simon and Garfunkel lyrics and remembered Chuck "trying to wrap each student in every cloak of knowledge he could create," but in the end she was excluded from his circle of favorites.

"I was a wallflower and he keyed in on students—I wouldn't say with higher intelligence because I was not stupid—but students who were more active, more aggressive with education. I remember him handing back a paper and saying it was excellent but I'm giving you a 'B' because you are a beta student. A grade based on social standing instead of the work. I remember walking away and being hurt. I thought, 'Maybe he really doesn't like me.' He was one of my favorite teachers until that day."

Chuck's freshness and audacity in bringing '60s culture into the classroom made him an immediate pop star to a legion of students. But there was a minority of skeptics like Al King who saw more sizzle than steak.

"I really liked Mr. Walls. But my perception was that he was absolutely a terrible teacher. The first day of school he was a mess and totally disorganized. Yet other students were having this amazing experience with him. I kept looking at it saying, 'Why do you *think* that?' For me, being a great teacher meant having substance. For them, it seemed they weren't talking about his teaching, they were talking about how he made them feel comfortable. 'Hey dude'...the anti-war thing...and maybe marijuana is not so bad. But it had nothing to do with teaching his class."

It was a seductive symbiosis between teacher and students. The more Chuck made them feel comfortable, the more they made him feel comfortable. And accepted.

The more he felt accepted, the more Chuck nurtured the affection of his students and deepened the alienation from his natural peer group, other teachers. He was oblivious to flashing caution lights.

"I did my best that fall to tell him what he had to do in order to continue to be a high school teacher," Blair said. "He was off to a bad start from the beginning because of his hair. I was a young teacher, too. I was straddling the line between being a teacher and the students. But nothing like he was. I told him, 'You're going to have to walk the walk when you're outside the classroom, and you gotta get your hair cut. Do what you need to do to 'fit in.' He didn't cut it. That symbolized to John Jones his rebellion."

Chuck kept marching to his own drummer, inside and outside the classroom. He kept raising the stakes, pushing bigger and bigger envelopes.

"I felt what got him on the radar wasn't the dope or even the long hair," King said. "It was his political point of view which he espoused in class. He wasn't a forceful communicator, but he would not be interrupted. 'Well, you may think that, but this is the other side of the issue and you need to hear this. Blah-blah-blah.' Those kids were going home and saying to their parents, this is what Mr. Walls is saying. That put him on the radar. Then the other pieces—smoking dope, having sex, all that shit— that's what killed him."

Blair watched helplessly as Chuck doubled-down on his rebellion.

"As the year wore on he had less and less support, and he would be called into the principal's office. He became the object of teasing and comments on the side. Don Beaver said to me, 'You have a relationship with him. I've tried to work with him. I'm very concerned. He's gonna get fired or have a lot of problems here if he doesn't shape up.'

"Regardless of my views about him personally, I really did feel that you had to make a sharp division between you and your students. You just couldn't do what he was doing and not pay a price and get away with it. I warned him and he didn't listen.

"I felt bad because the teachers had already judged him, sort of said early in the fall, 'He's not going to be one of us.' Who did it leave as a support group? No one. Either it's the teachers or the kids. When he closed his door he was at home, he had a group that hung on his every single word."

As the semester wore on "it became known he was inviting kids over to his apartment on the weekends and evenings," Rieger said. "A lot of parents who became aware of this raised the specter of Mr. Walls perhaps being a homosexual. And so the fire alarm went off.

"One night I came home really late, around midnight. My parents were in bed reading and asked me to come and sit down. We had a little discussion about their dislike of the situation and that potentially there could be a problem. They were as delicate as they could be because they didn't know, but at the same time they were being protective of their kids."

Roger Curry wore the black arm band and sometimes stayed after class to talk about war and politics with Chuck. He valued him as a beacon of truth in a sea of establishment "bullshit." And he feared for him.

"I don't think he even began to appreciate the dangerousness of what he was doing," Curry said. "If you don't conform on some level it's a very dangerous path."

Nowhere Man

*L*ike homing pigeons finding the way, safecrackers finding the combination, Columbo finding the clue—moms always find the diary.

"It was hidden but she found it," Jana Kellar said. "Moms are good at those things."

Kellar had sophomore English with Chuck and he was her chaperone for the Oxford summer that changed her and broke down the student-teacher wall between them. It was after the trip that Kellar began smoking dope. She and a few friends occasionally hung out with Chuck away from school. Kellar visited his apartment and he came to her home when her parents were not there.

Sometime in mid-October, Lucy Kellar's maternal divining rod pointed her to Jana's diary. She read it, put it back, and never told her daughter. Lucy died of cancer in 1971. "It was after my mom died that my dad told me she had read my diary," Kellar said.

Lucy, a registered nurse at Bloomington Hospital, and James Kellar, an IU anthropologist, were alarmed by Jana's diary but did not confront her immediately.

"My parents had, for that time, a very rational reaction when they found out I was hanging out with a teacher, doing drugs, doing all these kinds of things," she said. "They went to the family attorney to find out what the legal implications were, and they went to the family doctor and asked what the medical implications were of marijuana. They never mentioned Chuck's name."

It's a sign of those times that even a registered nurse in a university community knew so little about marijuana, still perceived by the great never-stoned majority as the evil weed of *Reefer Madness* horror flicks. As Don Beaver archly said of Chuck, "He was considered a drug addict. He smoked marijuana. How much worse can you get? We never knew there was anything worse than that."

Kellar said it was the family doctor or attorney who knew the lawyer for the school board. "He told him that one of his clients had a daughter with a problem and a school teacher was involved. The school board lawyer went, 'Chuck Walls.' So he was obviously on their radar. It was never my folks' intention to get Chuck in trouble. It was one of those things that just snowballed totally out of control."

Alerted by the board attorney, someone at BHS called the Kellars to ask about Jana's involvement with Chuck. The posse tracking Chuck did not see the diary and Kellar was never questioned, at least by officials. To satisfy their own need to know, Kellar's parents took her to Indianapolis for a private lie detector test, explaining vaguely that they 'found out' she was socializing with Chuck.

"I told the truth," she said.

By the end of October 1967 the board decided it had sufficient grounds to act. Chuck had felt the noose tightening since school began. "I remember him talking about how the administration did not like the way he was teaching," said Geoff Grodner, an *Optimist* staffer. "They did not like his longer hair. They didn't like anything about him. He was constantly butting heads with Jones."

"We knew that he was kind of a marked man," said a senior girl and member of a "little clique of misfits," core loyalists to whom he confessed a growing sense of peril.

The school board's Exhibit A was the allegation that Chuck had been at a student party in September where marijuana was used. On November 2 it voted to fire him, effective the 10th, unless exculpatory evidence was submitted before then. A meeting to review evidence was set for November 13. In the meantime, Chuck was banned from the school.

"He was just gone Monday," said John Fleener. "Somebody came in and took over his class and didn't discuss why he was gone. They made it really clear that he wouldn't be coming back. They said we were either getting a new teacher or a new teacher was already assigned. I can't remember. It was just very, very strange because things like that just don't happen."

Teachers were pumping students for information about their missing colleague. Peggy Pruett, an *Optimist* editor that year under Chuck, said one teacher "came up to me and said, 'Hey, what do you know about that guy? Do you know why he's suspended?' I said no, I don't know anything. Do you? He said no, no one does. 'They're keeping this hush-hush.' And then he made a derogatory comment—you know, no one liked Chuck."

High school students abhor a vacuum. Soon the halls were thick with rumors about Chuck's vanishing act. He was suspended for not cutting his hair. He was arrested for doing drugs. He had sex with a 15-year-old girl.

Whatever the reason, suspending a teacher in the middle of the school year was "really uncommon," said Bill Sturbaum, teacher union rep. "Rarely would that happen. I never remember another time. If he'd belonged to the union, I would have been there with him to make sure due process occurred."

For Deppe the rumors had substance. He had been to a party at Kellar's home where everyone including Chuck smoked dope. Though students had seen Chuck at other gatherings, that party was the school board's Exhibit A. Deppe came up with a plan to subvert the prosecution case, which relied on entries from Kellar's diary divulged by her parents.

Deppe's plan had a beautiful, time-tested simplicity—just lie—with a psychedelic twist.

"I told other people I knew who had been at the party that since Jana had been smoking pot and admitted it in her journal, we could testify that, yes, we had been at the party smoking pot but we never saw Chuck. Clearly, Jana must have been hallucinating."

Deppe was counting on the board's cluelessness about marijuana to swallow his risible *Reefer Madness* sequel. He wasn't disappointed.

"We were asked to testify, on the record, that we had been there and smoked pot and that Chuck wasn't there. We did this, I think, to the school board's attorney. There were four, five, six of us."

Deppe lied because "Chuck was a teacher that we loved. And it just felt like high school was too bleak a place to imagine his not being there. So I was willing to risk it."

Chuck retained James Cotner, a top Bloomington defense attorney, to make his case for reinstatement to the school board. But what happened next was proof of the generational aphorism about never trusting anyone over 30. Deppe and the others found out the hard way that it was not just a Chinese fortune cookie trying to be hip.

"We were assured that our testimony would be confidential, that it would not be turned over to police. That we were just making sure that justice was done for Chuck," Deppe said. "They turned over our testimony to the police. We felt utterly betrayed because our lies were not honored."

Not long after that, someone paid a surprise visit to the Deppe home, either a lawyer or a detective. Until that moment, Ted and Alice Deppe knew nothing of their son's risky business to rescue Chuck nor that he smoked dope.

"Whoever it was talked to my parents downstairs, then brought me upstairs to their bedroom and closed the door. He said I was in a lot of trouble. That I made this statement admitting I had used marijuana, that the police could make things very difficult for me, and they wanted me to help them bust the big people who were bringing drugs in to Bloomington from Chicago. This is how you can save yourself.

"I said, 'You're trying to turn me into a narc?' He said, no, you'd be doing the community a great service. I refused. My parents were heartbroken. It was a huge emotional thing for them. It seems to me that more than one student who lied for Chuck got some tough love from their parents. Mine were an example of unconditional love. They did not understand, they did not approve, and they stuck with me."

During his exile Chuck kept meeting in the shadows with his closest student friends. He was too mortified to tell his roommate that he was suspended. "He got up every morning, got dressed for school, and went to the IU library and read the *London Times,*" said Maudlin. "I learned about this later."

As suddenly as he had disappeared from school two weeks earlier, Chuck reappeared on November 15—but as a ghost of his recent self.

"When he came back he was so different," Pruett said. "Gone were the shaggy hair and long sideburns and the George Harrison ensemble. He left as the person who got off the plane from England. The day he came back he was back to the person he was before the trip. He had a dark suit, a white shirt and a skinny tie. And his hair was cut. He didn't really talk much after that."

"When he came back he was a whipped puppy," said Al King, a sophomore less enthralled than most with Chuck the teacher. "A different guy. A lot quieter. He didn't respond so much to some of the hippie-type kids who might go out and smoke dope with him."

Chuck returned under draconian conditions amounting to house arrest, expressed in a laundry-list of decrees. He was forbidden to speak about the Vietnam War except to support it. He was not to engage in any other controversial discussions. He was not to have discussions with students about other teachers. He was to keep both himself and his room neat and tidy. Administrators ordered him to straighten up and be a conservative teacher. They wanted nothing to disrupt the harmony of the building.

They wanted it to be 1966 again.

King was a Chuck skeptic from day one of the '67 fall semester. "I was used to very highly organized teachers and he wasn't any of those things. I left class the first day thinking, 'What the hell am I doing in here?'" During the suspension, "We did more work with the substitute than we did with him. I remember thinking, I need to stay away from this guy. He's dangerous. He was just calling too much attention to himself."

For King there was a moment that encapsulated what he regarded as Chuck's abdication of pedagogical authority in the classroom. It involved Janet Henry, a top student, the sort Chuck liked the best—an alpha.

"One day Mr. Walls gave us a writing assignment," King said. "Janet looked at him and said, 'Mr. Walls, I'm so sorry. I'm not going to do this assignment.' The class just stopped because she's not anyone who would ever do anything like that. He looked at her totally confused. 'Why not?' She said, 'I've given you seven assignments and I have no grades yet. I have not gotten any feedback on a paper, and until you do your job, I'm not doing this.'

"I have never seen anything come to such an abrupt halt. He looked like he'd been hit with a wet fish. He went over to his desk, sat down, straightened his hair a bunch of times, looked up and said, 'Fine, we'll just get this done.' He never looked up again. The next day all the papers came back to us. Very poorly graded. He handed them back quietly and left the classroom and never came back that day.

"No one said much. Janet was devastated because she did not mean to be disrespectful. She got up in front of class and said, 'I am so sorry. I did not intend for this to be the outcome.' I remember somebody saying the reason he didn't get the papers graded is that he spent all his time doing drugs. And everybody laughed.

"From that moment forward in the classroom he was stilted. And he was in trouble. And it just got darker and darker and darker."

This was not darkness, his old friend, that Chuck used to show how music and poetry "are one and the same" in the words of Scott Kragie. He recalled the day that Chuck, a fledgling teacher, began class by playing "The Sound of Silence," leaving the students stunned in silence and reflection.

That nurturing darkness was no kin to the toxic dark miasma slowly enveloping Chuck, just a year later. Looking back, Kragie realized that of all the music Chuck played in class he remembered only one song besides "The Sound of Silence." It was a lesser-known Simon and Garfunkel tune, "Richard Cory."

"Perhaps because," Kragie said, quoting Simon's lyric, 'Richard Cory went home last night and put a bullet through his head.'"

Not Your Mother's Tea Room

*T*he *Prisoner* was a TV series that debuted in England in 1967 and aired in the U.S. starting in June 1968. Starring Patrick McGoohan as a former spy abducted and held captive by unnamed sinister forces, it mirrored a growing sense of paranoia and powerlessness at the hands of authoritarian rulers and institutions in the real world.

It also served as an uncanny allegory for Chuck's predicament as it unfolded over the same period of time.

"In *The Prisoner*," wrote a British critic, "we witness a war of attrition between the faceless forces behind 'The Village,' a Kafkaesque community, and its most strong-willed inmate, No. 6 [McGoohan], who struggles ceaselessly to assert his individuality while plotting to escape from his captors."

Like No. 6, Chuck struggled ceaselessly to assert his individuality, was thwarted, punished, briefly banished, and by the end of 1967 was secretly plotting his escape from BHS. All the while he feigned acquiescence in strict new marching orders issued by his tormentors in the front office. He promised to dress appropriately. He expressed excitement about teaching *Twelfth Night* in class.

Over Christmas break, Chuck went to California to visit friends he had made in England, including Sue Bradbury. "We had a picture from his Christmas there: Chuck, Sue Bradbury and her father," said Sally. Chuck looked very much at ease. This was a place where he could live.

While there he interviewed at Menlo Park High School in the Bay area and accepted a job for the next school year as head of the journalism program, Sally said. Leaving the static midwest for the fluid ethos of California promised to be more than mere escape for Chuck. It would be fulfillment of a destiny interrupted, a lost soul delivered to its natural habitat. Chuck was a Hoosier who never seemed at home in his native state, or much interested in mollifying provincial blue noses.

From the start at BHS, Chuck flouted norms and taboos in sex, politics and drugs—minefields for teachers with an eye on job security. In the classroom he openly opposed the Vietnam War. Outside class he displayed a wanton disregard for discretion, fraternizing and smoking dope with students. By 1968 these behaviors were not secret in any real sense. They had become part of Chuck's persona among friends and enemies alike.

His violating the taboo against gay sex, on the other hand, was known only to a few. It was not something he readily shared or gloried in as part of his '60s' cloak like his Beatles haircut and rock and roll religion. No one did. In those days being queer ("gay" was not in the lexicon yet) was the third rail of taboos. Openly touching that rail could be fatal.

"Back then, even though the Kinsey Institute is there [at IU], nothing was talked about, nothing was open. If you were openly gay you were pretty guaranteed you would lose your job," said Wally Brazy, who student-taught at BHS.

"I think Chuck zeroed in on me because I was a sharp dresser, although I was dressing down so as not to seem gay. I was only wearing two patterns," Brazy deadpanned. "I remember in the staff room at Bloomington High there were two teachers—farmer-teachers I call them—in the same seats every day. The same white shirts, same black ties. To wear a light blue shirt would be too racy for them."

Chuck invited Brazy to observe his class. "It was a revelation. He was using songs as discussion points in English class, which was not done at all." Soon after that came an invitation to Chuck's apartment. They slept together a few times, Brazy said, prepared to "jump apart" when they heard straight arrow Maudlin at the door.

"I had just broken up with a boyfriend I was living with. Chuck had a boyfriend somewhere outside of Bloomington. Nothing had any permanence," Brazy said. "I knew people who broke up after one week because they'd been cheated on. That's how frantic it was. Two gay men who were together for a week would consider themselves married because that was such a long time."

Chuck was not the only gay teacher at BHS, just the most at risk because he kept pushing other hot buttons on drugs, politics and hair which spurred scrutiny and suspicion of all his activities. Would Chuck have been fired just for being gay?

"Not at all," said Blair, his friend and contemporary on the English faculty. "No, because they had Don Traub. My God."

If Chuck wanted a model for how to "pass" as a gay teacher, he had a tested one in Traub, the popular band director. Traub "passed" but not because anyone who passed him in the hall was fooled. Head held high, suit jacket flapping in his own breeze, the barrel-shaped Traub sailed through the halls like a Zeppelin. He and another man on the staff had a longtime relationship, Blair said.

"Oh, everyone knew. Were they sexual? Who knows. All I know is they traveled together every summer. It wasn't an issue. And part of it was, their behavior in school was appropriate."

Traub was a model for "go along to get along." Nobody cared he was gay, said track coach Goss, a culture warrior on the right who demanded rigid conformity from his athletes. "You just took it as, 'That's Don Traub.'

Don was at every athletic gathering there was after a game. He used to go with all the coaches and their wives."

Chuck never went along. He rarely visited the teacher lounge and never attended get togethers of the English faculty. He was the object of unrequited overtures from numerous female students who thought he was straight. "One student had a crush on Chuck and me," Brazy said. "I told her I was gay and so was Chuck. She goes, 'Oh, *that's* why we never kissed.'" Also disappointed was a boy who secretly coveted Chuck.

"I had no knowledge of Mr. Walls' sexuality," said Danny Higgins, "but I did have fantasies about him and tried to let him know how I felt, hinting that I wanted to be a close friend, hoping he would pick up on hints such as telling him, 'I really like *The Wizard Oz* and Judy Garland,' or, 'I'm glad to be a friend of Judy's.' Things that we did to fish for acknowledgement."

Higgins' feelers drew no response. "Was it my age and being a student? I don't think so since several female students told me they would go over to his apartment on the weekends. They all had crushes on him and hinted there was more going on than just talking. These girls were, shall we say, of the 'free soul' variety who all later became hippies."

Drum major and thespian, the exuberant Higgins occupied a pan-sexual netherworld of coursing teenage hormones and morphing identities. He dated girls ("I always had dates to dances because I could and would dance") and went steady for two years with the same girl, even as he made himself available to ostensibly straight classmates, many of them jocks.

"There was a lot of 'experimentation' by a large group of males on the down-low. The pill had not been invented so females were not so readily available to young guys who wanted to do more than masturbate. I helped a lot of them. There is an old joke that the only difference between a straight man and a gay man is a six pack of beer. I found that to be true and was very popular at certain cornfield parties.

"Someone would say they had to piss and ask me to accompany them and I knew what they really wanted. This would happen many times over the night with different guys. They would not be public friends and a few even put on like they hated me and wanted to beat me up. My low self-esteem at the time allowed them to behave that way without repercussions."

Cruising the same underworld on a parallel track was Al King, a gym-class stud with a straight aura who befriended coaches while remaining deeply closeted. There were some boys at BHS "so obviously gay they could not camouflage," he said. "Those guys were always my heroes. I respected that they couldn't camouflage and they had to be gay. I wish I could have been them."

King, who like Higgins also dated girls, had about 30 sexual encounters with male classmates, all away from school. "Some of them are still extremely well-known today," he said.

"I had lots of very comfortable liaisons with my straight friends who were athletes, and they were very happy to have those liaisons. There are a lot of straight guys who at that age don't know how to have sex. I was a safe place to have sex, and the next day we would act like it never happened. It really was the love that dared not speak its name. There was no talking about it. That's why we would have these wonderful nights then get up and everything was Aunt Jemima pancakes and bacon. It was the two worlds everybody had to live in."

King was born in Linton, a small coal-mining community 40 miles west of Bloomington. The high school teams were called The Miners. His dad was a miner. "I hated growing up in Linton. I just knew I wasn't supposed to be there." And he knew he was gay. "I didn't have a name for it, but I always knew. It was horrible."

Al King

Danny Higgins

[*Gothic* 1968]

Both problems, Linton and being gay there, were mitigated when King's dad quit the mines for health reasons and the family moved to Bloomington at the outset of junior high, and puberty, for King.

"One of the great places to be in the world if you were gay in the '60s was Bloomington because of the Kinsey sex research stuff. There were a lot of gay people on campus. Until I moved to Bloomington, I kinda thought I was the only gay person in the entire world. Then I found the campus. And I started having sexual interactions on campus, which was shocking to me, amazing. There are a lot of hang-out kind of bathrooms on campus and we jokingly called them tea rooms."

Higgins found the campus even earlier. It was his gateway to the cornfields. He discovered masturbation and fantasies at four years old and gave his first blow job at six. At 12 he was cruising the restroom at the courthouse on the square. By 14 he had discovered "the easy sex available on the campus at fraternity parties and the bathrooms in the Commons."

This was the same Commons, with the bowling alley and snack bar and tall windows looking out on Dunn Meadow where frat boys and "cutters" (sons of stonecutters) rumbled in *Breaking Away*. There were a few tables at one end of the low-ceilinged room that was an unofficial gathering place for gay students, Brazy said. "That's where you check in to see if anyone is having a party, what are other people doing."

Around the corner was the men's room, one of the biggest and busiest tea rooms on campus. "Some would go in the washroom and stay all day having anonymous sex," said Brazy, who thought the practice unwise. "People who start in washrooms end up in washrooms."

Chuck was no stranger to the washrooms. Like Paul Simon's boxer trolling Seventh Avenue, there were times when he was so lonesome he took some comfort there.

With a Little Help from My Friends

*S*ince almost everywhere else was so much worse, it's no exaggeration for Al King to say that in the '60s, Bloomington was "one of the great places in the world" if you were gay. But in citing the presence of the Kinsey Institute for Sex Research at Indiana University he misplaces the credit for making Bloomington a relative oasis of tolerance and safety for homosexuals.

A place for scholars to do scientific research, the institute did not offer programs and lectures for students or the public (tours did not start until 2000) nor did it provide counseling or therapy for sexual dysfunction. It did have the occasional "date night" for staffers featuring selections from the institute's collection of "incredible pornographic films," said Dean Hartley, a graduate student who was paid $6 an hour to proofread manuscripts.

For the Bloomington beyond campus, the Kinsey Institute had less impact than IU dental researchers who provided free toothpaste, brushes and checkups to 2,000 local schoolchildren while developing Crest with fluoride in the '50s. A grade-school classmate, Geoff Grodner, gifted with a toothy smile, starred in one of the iconic Crest commercials with the punchline, "Look, Mom, no cavities!"

For all its notoriety and ground-breaking research, the Institute was not the engine of sexual enlightenment (look, Mom, no depravities!) which over time would make Bloomington/IU "a haven for LGBT communities...an anomaly," in the words of a thesis by IU graduate Solomon

Hursey. In 1969, Bloomington had the second largest chapter of the Gay Liberation Front in America, behind New York and ahead of San Francisco, Hursey said.

Credit for the anomaly properly belongs to the man who midwifed the Kinsey Institute against all odds and pitchfork opposition—IU president Herman B Wells. Alfred Kinsey's *Sexual Behavior in the Human Male*, published in 1948, was to sexology what Stephen Hawking's *A Brief History of Time* was to cosmology. Wells is the first person named in the acknowledgments after the 5,300 anonymous males who shared their sexual histories.

That the most influential book of the 20th century about human sexuality, sort of a manual for the sexual revolution, was researched and written not at Harvard or Columbia or Cambridge, but at a state university in southern Indiana, is as wildly improbable as a music school the equal of Juilliard materializing in the same place—which is yet another instance of Wells' sorcery.

Raised in small-town Indiana, Wells shaped IU into a leading research university and cosmopolitan center of culture. In 25 years as president (1937-62), he was a constant quiet crusader against all varieties of bigotry, on campus and off. Wells died in 2000 at age 97. The *New York Times* obituary noted, "He defended Dr. Alfred C. Kinsey, the head of the Institute for Sex Research at the university, against calls for his dismissal, and argued for the right of scholars to pursue their quest for truth without harassment."

The obituary greatly understated the reach of Wells' advocacy for tolerance on issues of sexuality. Unbeknownst to the *Times*, and to virtually anyone not directly affected, were his discreet efforts to shield the secreted gay community at IU from persecution. That, at least, was the perception of many gay men and women at IU in the '60s.

"We were protected by Chancellor Wells," said Brazy. "He was sort of our patron saint, the one who would keep the police at bay. They were trying to harass people and he told them to lay off. To stay out of the university. We knew we were pretty safe on campus."

John Hartley (no relation to Dean) came to IU in 1963 as a graduate student. "I was not exactly gay and not exactly *not* gay." Either way, he soon became acquainted with the tea rooms on campus.

"About 1965 an over-zealous student organization called the Board of Aeons, which is supposed to have some role offering the university guidance from the students' viewpoint, became annoyed and horrified that there was so much cruising going on in the Union Building and in the main library. Cameras were installed in the toilet in the basement of the library because it was the notorious one. It was very big, five or six stalls.

"When Wells found out about this he was horrified. He said he had never heard of such an invasion of privacy, that it was outrageous, and he had them removed immediately. I always heard this story. It was not in the newspapers, but I believe it to be true. It's totally consistent with Wells' personality. He was deeply humane and tolerant and would never have wanted anything like that."

Hartley had a gay friend from high school, Don Buttram, who went by the name "Elvira" at IU. He was working on his master's in history when a tea room visit went awry.

"He was having sex with some guy in a toilet, and lo and behold, one of his professors walked in and caught him *in flagrante*. The professor went to the dean of students and reported it. Elvira was called in and was told he was going to be expelled. I can't remember if one of us said you should go to Chancellor Wells and ask for mercy and act contrite, but he did. Elvira wasn't stupid.

"And Wells said—this is what Don Buttram told me—'I need to have your oath that you won't get yourself in trouble like this again. If I'm going to go to bat for you, I don't want to be made a fool of.' And he said, 'Oh, I swear.' I don't know if that was a promise he could really keep. Who after all can make promises never to have sex? Anyway, Wells fixed it all up. And Don got this letter telling him that thanks to Herman Wells saying he had an interest in this case, and was willing to work with you, we are going to forget these allegations, or something like that."

The stories of Wells intervening on behalf of gay students in distress may be truth or legend or some hybrid. But like the mystery of his own sexual orientation, it didn't matter. Perception was reality for gay men and women at IU in the '60s. They believed, *needed* to believe, the stories to be true.

Short and stout with an elfin mien and Cheshire grin, Wells had the perpetual look of a man holding a winning poker hand. His sexuality was as unfathomable as his Svengali-like knack for making friends and reassuring leery conservatives in the state capitol, the business community, and small-town Rotary clubs. Like Churchill's description of Russia, his sexuality was "a riddle wrapped in a mystery inside an enigma."

Wells never married and lived in the president's house in the heart of campus with a succession of "house boys," IU students who served as chef, chauffeur and companion. Most people assumed Wells was gay, some thought he was asexual. No one cared either way.

"Everyone has always thought that Wells was gay and I'm sure he was…I think," laughed John Hartley. "A lot of his house boys were gay. I knew various ones. But I never heard any of them say that they knew him having had sex with a boy or a man. He wasn't in the closet, he was in a vault. I've always had the feeling that the fact he was secretly gay probably gave him a reason to like what Kinsey was doing because he saw it as steps toward a liberation that could only be vaguely imagined then."

Wells' furtive efforts for a lucky few in the '60s belied the fact that equal treatment for homosexuals at IU still lay on a far horizon. Closets remained full. Job security was an issue. In 1961 a popular professor of Spanish tried to kill himself by walking into traffic the day after he was charged with mailing obscene material—pictures of nude men—through the mail. Wells vouched publicly for Glen Willbern's character, but he was convicted and dismissed from the university.

One graduate student said it took "almost forever" to complete a master's in education "because a homophobic instructor gave me an 'F' in a simple, required statistics course. It took about 40 school hours of straight 'A's to bring my average up to a 'B' required for my master's. In those days we had no voice to object to such treatment."

Dean Hartley was a Ph.D. candidate in English and did not feel free to write a dissertation that reflected his orientation and interest in gay culture.

"No one would have accepted it, no one would have worked with me on it," he said. "It would have compromised them. They might have advised me to do an article on 'Billy Budd: Fag or Fairy?' and send it to the *Atlantic Monthly*, but they wouldn't have been my advisor on that sort of dissertation."

Malcolm Brown was a closeted gay husband and father when he joined the IU faculty in 1961 as a musicologist. His daughters' Girl Scout leader was Clara Kinsey, Alfred's wife. "Ranger Kinsey as we called her." Brown and his wife separated in 1967, but he was cruising tea rooms before that. On occasion he crossed paths with colleague Jorge Bolet, a renowned piano virtuoso.

"He used to cruise in the Union Building," Brown said. "I would go in one of those restrooms and there would be Jorge Bolet standing at the urinal. Every now and then you would hear about somebody getting caught, and it was pretty dire. I was terrified that I would get caught. On the other hand, I felt the need so strongly that I'd still do it. I was never caught."

Not everyone was so lucky. "I remember an opera coach who was discovered in some sort of compromised position, I guess by the police, and it was reported to Bain," Brown said, meaning music dean Wilfred Bain. "I was told, and it was plausible then, that Bain called this man into his office and said, 'I want you out of town by Monday. I don't want to see you in the School of Music. I'll call the police if you're here. Get out.'"

There was gay social life outside the tea rooms, though equally sub rosa.

"Wealthy gays had fabulous parties, but they weren't open to the public," said Dean Hartley. "A lot of undergraduates were to be found at them. The only criteria were looks and wit, though prominence on campus also counted. I slept with just about everybody I wanted to—faculty, administration, politicos, townspeople, students—and had large parties for visiting faculty and writers. Several lovers were fraternity presidents or big shots. One was a champ jock. For a year I slept with a vice president of the university. He was terribly afraid someone was going to find out."

The gay social underground was enlivened by other characters like "Elvira" with colorful stage names: "Moonflower," a queen from the Philippines, and "Perverta Gray," both denizens of the Hide-a-Way Cafe just off campus; and "Rhoda the Roach," named for the cockroach in *Archy and Mehitabel*, smart-aleck cartoon characters in the work of a New York columnist in the early 1900s. Rhoda favored big hats from *Breakfast at Tiffany's* and *My Fair Lady*, and false eyelashes and rouge. His iconic party moment was the night he gave birth to a rubber dolly.

In 1967, *The Indiana Daily Student* published an unsigned short story by Dean Hartley about the gay subculture at IU which caused a sensation and triggered police surveillance of The Fireside, a popular restaurant-bar in town.

The whimsical satire was based on Hartley's knowledge of "the under-cover gay community of fraternity guys, jocks, and TA's (teacher assistants) who dated their sorority girlfriends, took them back to the houses, then zoomed over to the Fireside for gay socializing. Along with the Royal Oaks it was one of the few public venues in those days that gays could frequent."

Indiana Avenue running along the west side of campus was the busiest border between town and gown. Gay students crossing the border onto Kirkwood Avenue, city territory, were no longer in Chancellor Wells' sphere of influence and protection. In those days, before the 1969 Stonewall riots at a gay bar in New York which led to establishing the Gay Liberation Front, Bloomington was not the "haven for LGBT communities" it would someday become.

"Despite the fact hippies were all over the place and everybody smoked dope, and the general admonition was 'put it where it feels good,' it was still very macho," said John Hartley. "Men were very resentful of gay men just for identifying themselves as gay. If they sat at the bar at Nick's English Hut to cruise, bartenders would notice and they didn't like it. It offended them on a moral basis. [In 1971 Nick's posted a sign stating: "This Is Not A Fruit Stand!"] "And back then it was like spittin' on niggers. It may not be a very nice thing to do, but no one is going to call you on it. Because everyone understands that, well, naturally you just spit on niggers, and you spit on gay people."

Gay men weary of the tea room scene cruised high-risk areas downtown, right under the nose of police. Some had sex in the bushes around the courthouse, Hartley said. The main cruising ground was the library a block from the square. "The street lights were much dimmer then," he said. "The trees were much denser. And there weren't as many parking lots."

Ross Allen, a renowned opera director at IU, devised an ingenious survival strategy. "I used to see Ross out roaming the streets at night," Hartley said.

"When he cruised he always carried a letter. If anyone caught him on the street, like a colleague or anybody at all, he would say he was on his way to the post office to mail a letter. It was a joke that he always carried a letter."

There was no gay bar, per se, in Bloomington. But the Royal Oaks, just off the west side of the square, evolved into what might be called a bi-bar. "It was a nice bar, wood-paneled and everything," said Dean Hartley. In the afternoon the clientele was mostly straight stoners—stonecutters just off work—and a larger group of "stonies," west-side and rural locals. "From about 8 till closing it was gay. Some nights like Saturday it was almost all stoners out spending their hard-earned dough. They apparently never washed so most gays were not tempted to pick them up."

Gays were comfortable at the Royal Oaks because it hired a couple of gay bartenders, said John Hartley. "One of them was named Rich. Boy, was he something. He was this big tall guy with bulging muscles, wore tight T-shirts. He was an archer and sometimes wore this leather thing on his arm. Some of the gay guys used to look at that and just get shivers."

The Royal Oaks was a place "where you might meet people who could be considered 'rough trade,' less sophisticated. Like a truck driver might be rough trade, or a steel worker," said longtime gay resident Gary Pool.

Closeted gay faculty were more likely to frequent Sully's Oaken Bucket, a more genteel, ostensibly straight restaurant on the other side of the square. "I had dinner there one time with some friends who were gay and there were gay faculty there, but they were embarrassed to see us because they didn't want to be known," said Dean Hartley.

No one remembers seeing Chuck at a fabulous gay party, in the courthouse bushes or at Sully's incognito. The one gathering place for gay men where Chuck was seen was the tea room in Jordan Hall at IU. It was one of the safer tea rooms on campus, said Al King, an habitué himself when he was at BHS.

"Getting caught there is pretty hard to do because when you open the door it doesn't open right into the area with stalls. There's a hallway and you can hear people coming," King said. "The way it works is, you're in the stalls. You close the door but there's a crack where you can see out."

King recalled the first time he saw his English teacher in the tea room.

"I was seated where I could see who was coming in, and it was Chuck. There's a lot of stalls and he went down to the very end and had sex with a guy in the stall. I knew that because as I leaned over to look you could see them having sex. You could see their feet together. So there's no doubt about it.

"It actually happened twice. I saw him that time, and then the second time he was going in as I was going out, and he had this terrible shocked look on his face. And I think at that point we both knew. After that he looked at me even less in class. It was like I was invisible. He knew I was dangerous."

La Petite Coquette and The Big Mushroom

*W*hen Chuck Walls met Myriam Champigny in the late '60s, it was a convergence of alien worlds. Local high school teachers and French wives of existential poets didn't run in the same circles. The lines of social demarcation were bright red and rigid: town and gown, blue collar and tweed, catfish and caviar, Grand Ole Opry and high opry.

The '60s changed that in university communities like Bloomington, ripe (in Leonard Cohen's phrase) with "the spiritual thirst" for a new world. Political tumult over Vietnam, revolutions in sex, drugs and music, and the incipient liberation of blacks, women and gays all flowed together in a tide eroding the boundaries between gender, race, class and culture.

Charles Ancil Walls, the son of a Methodist pastor from Evansville, Indiana, and Myriam Cohen Champigny, the daughter of a diplomat/novelist from Marseille, France, met at her home on leafy Maxwell Lane. Myriam (mee-ree-AHM) and her husband, Robert (ro-BARE) shared their home a few blocks from the IU campus with more cats than anyone could count. "La Maison des Chats" one acquaintance called it.

Chuck and Myriam were introduced by his college roommate, Alan Thomas who met Myriam on campus when she was signing up people for animal rescue work. Thomas found her entirely charming and thought Chuck would, too.

Myriam was a teacher, photographer, irrepressible free spirit, tireless social butterfly, and unabashed coquette. She and Robert were models for the notion of opposites attracting. He was saturnine, reclusive, taciturn. "The big mushroom," a friend, Ginny Peacock, playfully called Robert, linking Champigny to champignon, French for mushroom. It was an apt pairing: both the poet and the fungi thrived in dim isolation.

Thomas, a desultory student who majored in sybarite studies ("sex, drugs and rock 'n' roll") remembers making the fateful introduction, in late 1967 or early '68 as Chuck was nearing his desperate hours. Myriam was 47, Chuck half her age. The ostensible reason for their meeting was Chuck's interest in animals, but "he could have given a shit about animal welfare," said Thomas.

The Animal Rescue League (ARL) was set up as an alternative to the Humane Society shelter which was "run by two horrible old people, a couple, like something dredged up from a swamp," said Ann McGarrell, a poet and founding mother of the ARL. "Every time you saw them you would just pray they would get rectal cancer, which I believe he did."

The society employed "vicious, venal peasants" and kept stray animals caged with their own feces for days and weeks, she said. "They were selling cats to the army and Windsor Biology Gardens," an outfit which bought the cats and resold them at farmers markets. "We would go to the godforsaken so-called *Humane* Society building and say, 'Oh, that's my cat' and give them $3."

The ARL was mostly faculty wives like McGarrell whose artist husband, Jim, directed the graduate painting program at IU. It also attracted a smattering of students. The ARL maintained a shelter for rescued cats on 20 acres outside Bloomington and ran its own adoption program. Thomas put in many hours alongside Myriam cleaning kennels, changing litter, scrubbing floors. For some student volunteers it was just too real.

"They had great trouble with the grotty side of rescue," said Roger Lass, an ARL co-founder. "It's a bit hard getting into the routine of handling shit and vomit. I remember particularly one girl who was very devoted but decided she couldn't do it any longer when a cat she was petting puked up a handful of roundworms."

One student who came to ARL meetings for a while was a Chi Omega sorority girl, Emily Harris, who student-taught at Binford Junior High and later switched from rescuing cats to kidnapping newspaper heiresses. With husband Bill, also an IU grad, she joined the Symbionese Liberation Army, a leftist group that abducted Patty Hearst. No one recalls Chuck attending ARL meetings, much less cleaning kennels. His involvement seems to have been limited to helping Myriam with mailing lists. But the paperwork produced a toxic bond.

It was the oddest of mutual attractions. Neither side was drawn to the other sexually. Yet, La Maison des Chats became a home away from home to which Chuck returned time and again to Myriam until, finally, it became the scene of their mutual destruction.

By all accounts, Myriam was irresistible, an ageless ingenue with appeal to gay, straight and all shadings between. "Myriam was innocent. She always looked like a little girl. She never looked like a lady," said Shehira Davezac, a neighbor and friend. "Even at her age, fortysomething, she looked 22," said Ann McGarrell. Myriam was physically alluring, "a Brigitte Bardot lookalike" in the eyes of a straight male friend.

"She was my height exactly, 5-1, with beautiful round breasts and a tiny bum," said McGarrell, a close friend and occasional travel companion in Europe. "We could wear each other's clothes. But her dresses were ample on top and my pants were too big for her. We were sort of reversely shaped. Together we would have been the perfect woman."

Myriam worshipped the sun like a college spring breaker. "She had this amazing bone structure and skin despite tanning far too passionately,"

Myriam Champigny in her garden circa 1967 [Courtesy of Alan Thomas]

McGarrell said. "Even in Switzerland she used fold-out tanning boards. She was very much a sun child."

Myriam had a magnetic personality "that you were madly attracted to," said Thomas, who had his first gay sexual encounter in her home. "If you were doing a portrait to illustrate effervescence, you would not show a glass of Alka-Seltzer, you would show Myriam," said McGarrell. "She had that gift of being silly."

Another gay friend remembers her as "a tiny, ultra-liberal cat lady who fancied herself sort of feline. She liked to dress up in drag with cat's-face makeup. She was really cute and utterly charming. She filled the heads of anyone who would listen with the forlorn poetry of the 19th century, in contrast to the bleak, dry cynicism of post-war existentialism that was the specialty of her husband."

For a short time, Myriam taught beginning French at IU in a non-faculty position. Virginia Berry had transferred from a small college to IU for its superior foreign language program which she heard included native French instructors. She got her wish and was placed in Madame Champigny's class. Whatever she expected the first day of class, it wasn't Myriam.

"I was stunned by her. She looked like the stereotypical little gamine. Short hair, small-boned, little face. She always had on something wonderful like a mohair sweater, clothes we didn't have. European clothes, I guess. She wore little shoes, sling-back heels that were low, and she would fly around the room like a little butterfly that would light on things and then move on to the next. And all the time she's talking in French, and she spoke so that you could get it. She was a good teacher."

One morning Myriam flew into class in her little shoes exultant over new fallen snow on campus, Berry said. "It was pretty and the sun was out and she was rattling off in French how lovely it was and what a treat it was to see the snow and how she heard people *complaining* that it got their hair wet. And she did that mouth like Marcel Marceau, an upside down U."

It was difficult for anyone of any orientation with a beating heart and libido not to fall for Myriam. Chuck's attraction to Myriam was more complex. It seemed to spring from a deeper place, a starved region of his psyche as a closeted gay man. Myriam satisfied a need in him more gnawing and urgent than sex: unconditional acceptance.

She had done the same for Thomas the night he confided to her that he might be gay. "Of course you're gay," Myriam said.

"She was so nonjudgmental," said Thomas. "She instilled freedom in people. She brought them alive. I knew people who were so into being an intellectual, being hot shit. You'd introduce them to Myriam and two weeks later they would be out flying a kite. I mean that literally. She would say, 'Why are you so uptight? You've got to live your life...have a good time.' She would break the chains and bonds to allow you to be you."

In her words could be heard echoes of Timothy Leary at Golden Gate Park, chanting the trademark mantra of the '60s social revolution: "Turn on, tune in, drop out." Chuck had turned on and tuned in but had no wish to drop out and fly kites, only to escape the chains of secrecy and shame which bound him. Myriam was there with the key to say, "What is the big issue here?"

Perhaps her *joie de vivre* and passion to share it like a joint of fine weed flowed from the joy of escaping a wrenching past. Her mother died when she was three. At 19, the Nazis came. Her father Albert Cohen—novelist, playwright, diplomat—was brilliant but self-absorbed.

"Albert Cohen was a genius and madly charming but also a spoiled brat," said McGarrell. "He didn't write his novels, he dictated them to whatever enthralled woman happened to be in his life at that moment. [The wives alone numbered three.] He was this huge egomaniac. Very demanding."

Belle du Seigneur, a comic romance novel considered Cohen's masterpiece, would come much later. ("Robert never liked his father-in-law's writing," said Davezac. "He thought his books were ghastly.") But when the war began Cohen had already achieved sufficient literary celebrity from his early work to be included on the Nazis' list of most-wanted Jews.

"Albert Cohen's publisher, Gallimard, had heard somehow that the Nazis were coming for him," said McGarrell. "It was Gaston Gallimard himself who came to warn them that they were about to be arrested and needed to get out of Paris immediately. They were able to get a boat to England with Myriam's stepmother, Marianne, carrying Myriam's kitten in her sable muff. There was a quarantine on animals coming into England, but Myriam was so beautiful she just flashed the kitten at the customs officer and he said, 'I didn't see that.'"

Robert Champigny (shahm-pee-NEE) grew up in Chatellerault some 200 miles south of Paris. The family was poor. "His father was a mean-spirited old peasant," McGarrell said. Robert was rescued by his natural gifts. "Football and bicycle races were the ticket out of poverty for a bright young country boy. He went off to the Sorbonne in sabots [simple shoes]. His father gave him his own hat."

Robert joined the resistance while still a student. "He heard his classmates being tortured while a loud recording of Beethoven's 'Ode to Joy' covered their screams," McGarrell said. "He escaped by hanging outside his window by his fingertips while his room was searched, then later hid for weeks in a field of Jerusalem artichokes."

Robert fled to England and it was there he met Myriam. "When he and Myriam found each other in London they were like lost children," McGarrell said. Both worked for Radio Free France, which broadcast to occupied France from studios of the BBC. After the war they returned to France and Robert taught English at lycées in Chartres and Saint Germaine-en-Laye. They were married in October 1948.

"Myriam painfully lost a baby in childbirth," McGarrell said. "The baby was born but died instantly and the French doctors and nursing staff would not let her hold it, and told her it was her own fault for having a small pelvis. She once told me she had decided not to have the baby in France because Robert would look at her widening body and weep. She preferred to go away, have the baby—to be named Robin—return and present him with a fait accompli."

In September 1950, Robert and Myriam boarded Cunard's RMS Caronia in Havre, France, for New York, a journey of one week. On the ship manifest their destination in the U.S. was listed as "Indiana University, Bloomington, Ind.," indicating Robert had already secured his position at IU as French instructor. They carried five pieces of luggage plus emotional baggage.

"They were two gorgeous, very skinny people, both with impossible fathers and stepmothers," McGarrell said. "They had passed through horrors and were ready for a new life. They brought the carefully packed Baccarat wine glasses that had been [writer] Annette Vaillant's wedding gift to them, and a bottle of Marc."

At IU, Robert steadily ascended the faculty ladder from instructor to research professor of French. Along the way he published 15 books of literary-philosophical criticism and wrote seven volumes of poetry. His most notable work, published in 1959, was *Sur un Heros Paien* (*A Pagan Hero*), a study of Camus. In 1964 he won the Durchin-Louvet Prize for "outstanding contributions to French letters and literature," given each year to a Frenchman living abroad who has helped promote his home-land's culture.

Hédi Bouraoui, a noted Tunisian-Canadian writer and academic, studied under Robert as a graduate student. One day early in 1960 he encountered his professor in a busy hallway of Ballantine Hall, the largest classroom building on campus. Robert, who maintained an air of regal prepossession befitting a man lost in existential thought, was highly animated that day. He was holding a sheet of paper.

"He said, 'Hédi, come here, come here. I want to talk to you!' We get in a corner and he says, 'Do you know what happened?' I said no. 'Camus died. And I received a letter from him one week after his death, as if he is writing to me from his grave.' So he starts reading the letter. Camus is telling him that his book (*A Pagan Hero*) is the best book ever written about *The Stranger*. Both of us were crying like babies, tears were in our eyes."

Robert apparently believed that such emotion and animation had no place in the classroom. He did not flit around the room. His pedagogical style was sit and deliver. "He was not a very good teacher because he wrote his lecture and read it," Bouraoui said. "He didn't lecture like me. I get up and talk. He sat in the chair and read his lecture. He asked us to ask him questions about what he said, and we did. He was very good in answering questions, but he was not very good at ad-libbing."

Like the Great Sphinx, what Robert lacked in spontaneity he made up in heroic profile and mystery. If Myriam was the stereotype gamine, Robert was Hollywood's pipe-smoking French poet-philosopher: dark-eyed, brutally handsome despite a retreating hairline, his angular frame honed by soccer, tennis and bike riding. "He spoke English with a French accent: 'The prob-LIM we are talking ah-BOAT.' The Americans find it very charming," Bouraoui said.

Virginia Berry never had Robert for class but met him one day on campus. He had her at "Bonjour."

"I just about fainted. He was something to behold. He went around wearing these fantastic fishermen's sweaters with the big thick turtlenecks, often black, and he had dark hair and his nose was large. Imagine a cartoon of a Frenchman—he had everything but the beret. He walked around with this semi-scowl. It was terribly attractive."

Robert Champigny circa 1967 [Courtesy of Hédi Bouraoui]

At ARL meetings Robert "would sit in the corner looking saturnine, and every time a problem came up he would suggest, in his hugely thick French accent, 'write a check,'" said Lass. Though distant and brooding, Robert was no snob. He often wore bicycle shorts in his office. He played soccer and rode bikes with neighborhood kids.

"He had long periods of melancholy, out of which I really believe he escaped through sport," McGarrell said. "Myriam once saw him playing soccer with some kids and said, 'Isn't it amazing how men disappear into sport? They just become something else.'"

Robert was an ambitious and solitary gardener, spending hours in the backyard with Chafou by his side. "He was like a child in many ways," said Davezac. "He had a child's imagination, building miniature castles in the garden."

Robert's devotion to Camus was exceeded only by his bond with Chafou (Shah-foo). "A deep reciprocal passion" McGarrell called it. Long- haired with a striped brow and stony stare, Chafou "looked like a cat that belonged to Marie Antoinette." Myriam found him in the Alps on one of her visits home, McGarrell said.

"Myriam was hiking with her former step-mother and they saw a hawk swooping down, circling, and they thought, 'Oh, it's a deer or a rabbit. We should chase the hawk away.' When they got up there it was this beautiful, long-haired cat. Apparently, he was so gregarious he had followed hikers up from the village. He was really starved. They put him in their rucksack and took him down to where they were staying and fed him. He was so self-possessed, he was not just beautiful."

Soon the cat was on a plane to America. McGarrell went with Robert to pick up Chafou.

"Robert got this telegram saying, 'Cat arriving Indianapolis airport. Such and such flight. Don't worry - cat well.' The flight got in quite late, via

New York, maybe 11 o'clock at night. The cat arrived in a very delicate little wicker basket that the French carry with a wire grill in front. Tied to the handle was a note that said, 'My name is Chafou and I like to be fed bits of steak by fingers.' Robert had to pay the customs person overtime to come back and check the cat through."

Myriam busily carved out her own niche in Bloomington. Years before her gig at IU, she began a pilot program at University School to teach French in the early grades. She was a gifted and prolific photographer, developing her own film for black-and-white portraits of nudes, Robert and Chafou, visiting dignitaries such as poet Robert Fitzgerald, and neighbor kids including Heidi Remak—a future student of Chuck's—and her three brothers who lived down the street.

They had parties from time to time, despite Robert's social reticence, and were aficionados of American pop culture. "Myriam loved Bob Dylan and TV shows like *Mission Impossible*," said McGarrell. "Robert loved American noir movies and detective stories, especially Raymond Chandler, in part because Chandler had an adored black cat in one of his book jacket photos."

There was one thing about Robert which seemed anomalous, an errant brush stroke in the portrait of a man devoted to poetic truth, beauty and the life of the mind. It was a detail out of sync with the Baccarat wine glasses and Marc and ornamental gardening; with the serenity of a street not far from campus where he and Myriam lived among the like-minded.

Robert kept a .38 caliber handgun in his desk drawer.

Those who knew him best were not entirely surprised. He had fits of melancholia that went beyond the occupational hazard of an existentialist.

"Robert was a man of few words," said Davezac. "He did get into dark moods. The gun gave him comfort to know that if it was really terrible, he could end it."

"He had lived through the Gestapo," McGarrell said. "He'd had friends tortured to death by the Nazis. I think he wanted to be able to kill himself if he wanted to. He never said that. But Myriam was always afraid that because of his great leaps of temperament it was something that could happen."

Bridge Over Troubled Water

*I*n the 1950s and '60s many of Bloomington's business and academic elite—deans and industrialists, doctors and quarry owners, artists and salesmen, a Nobel laureate—lived in an area just south and east of downtown, less than a mile from the IU campus. It's known as Vinegar Hill, named for the odor of rotting apples from the orchards that once thrived there.

Dating from the 1920s, these were the grandest homes in Bloomington with an eclectic array of Tudor and Colonial Revival, Greek Revival, French Provincial, Spanish Colonial, Italian Renaissance and Art Deco. Indiana limestone was used in many homes, evident in carved relief friezes and gargoyle drains, the handiwork of local artisans. Alfred and Clara Kinsey lived here in a red brick house with a steeply sloped A-shaped roof that he designed. In back was a large garden where he cultivated irises and day-lilies.

Just two streets but several income brackets away, on the periphery of Vinegar Hill, was Maxwell Lane, lined with boxy ranch-style houses occupied by a broad range of middle-class from town and gown. Robert and Myriam's home was unremarkable but carried a rare distinction. It was a Lustron home.

In the late '40s an Ohio inventor, eyeing the post-war housing shortage, patented a process for using steel to make affordable, low-maintenance homes. He succeeded on both scores. But production costs were astronomical and Lustron folded in 1950. In all, Lustron produced 2,498

Myriam and Robert Champigny outside Bloomington home, circa 1958 [Courtesy of Myriam Champigny website]

homes, including 159 in Indiana. The Champignys' was one of five in Bloomington.

Myriam and Robert were aesthetically appalled by the colorless, pre-fabricated porcelain-enameled steel panels on the exterior of the house. It looked like they were living in a vault with windows. They hired a builder to cover up the outrage.

"It was in a very rustic style of brick-laying with the mortar squished out," said Robert Fichter, a friend and master photographer. "When I asked Myriam—as that sort of thing was not common in Indiana—she said it was a reminder of her childhood, and that the builder laid the brick himself because he did not want his brick layer to develop a bad habit. The midwest is neat and clean, you know."

The face-lifted ranch would be further transformed by a large addition, another homage to the homelands the couple never completely left behind. "They had this marvelous little chateau in back. You'd think you were in Switzerland," said Alan Thomas. "The bottom was Myriam's art studio and the top was a large room all paneled in pine with a big fireplace."

Less clear is what went on inside the Lustron walls and chateau. Dope smoking? Sexual liaisons among visitors? The answer depended on who was talking, and whether they visited when the professor was home or out of town lecturing, as he frequently was.

At home Robert spent long hours in his study absorbed in composition. "He would write constantly. You could hear him on the typewriter," Davezac said. Myriam often "would get into bed early and read. She would be doing nothing. Robert wasn't very social. The minute he would leave, Myriam would be another person. A motorcycle would come and the neighbors were there."

When Robert was away, the ambience at 1040 morphed from writer's garret to Hotel California with a lot of pretty, pretty boys Myriam called friends. "Myriam was a fag hag *ante litteram* [before its time]," McGarrell said. "She admired ambiguity and outsiderness which God knows is a huge theme in French literature."

Once in Robert's absence, Myriam was whisked away on motorcycle to a secret gay or drag "wedding" in the basement of the stately Graham Hotel downtown, complete with Cristal Champagne. The "bride" is said to have worn a white wedding dress borrowed from the window of Wick's department store on the square.

"Myriam had different circles of friends," said Alan Thomas. "She behaved differently with each circle. She was a professor's wife married to a very famous writer and intellectual. She ran with those groups. Then she had the bottom group. I think I was the top rung of the bottom group. That was her other life, her gay friends. I really think she was freer with her gay friends."

Whatever her own preferences may have been, Myriam, as hostess, offered a tolerance and welcome mat for sexual adventurers that reflected the evolving "free love" ethos of the '60s. One friend said she "provided a manner of *salon* for gay men" plus a "dominatrix queen," wife of a faculty member.

"Myriam used to let lots of people use her house for having sex," said John Hartley. "College students didn't have apartments back then very often. It wasn't permitted for undergraduates. So she was just being nice, obliging friends."

She was equally obliging to guests wishing to fire up a fatty, and eager to inhale. "She *liked* smoking grass," said Hartley. "I remember she kind of smelled like grass a lot of the time. She was not a dope peddler or anything like that." Thomas had the same impression. "I never knew her to have any marijuana in her house. Whenever I would go to her house I would always take it."

One night, Thomas said, "I was sitting on the floor of Myriam's bedroom and we were smoking pot when my father killed himself. My car was in the garage, so I borrowed her car to drive home to Brazil. When I drove in the driveway it was full of police and ambulances and squad cars. They said he had shot himself."

Davezac, who lived just two streets away with her husband, Bernard, an IU art history professor, had no inkling that her good friend enjoyed marijuana as well as fine wine. "I really don't think it played any role in her life, drugs. Not at all," she said. "Experimentally, it might have been fun for her to try."

McGarrell assumed that Myriam did use weed on more than an experimental basis but, "She never smoked it in front of me. Not because she thought I was straight, and not because I didn't think it was charming. She knew I couldn't inhale anything."

It seemed that Myriam abstained from burning joints around McGarrell for the same reason she made her home available for assignations: kindness and consideration.

One of the larger pot-laced parties at the Champigny compound featured a special guest—Marianne Goss. She was Albert Cohen's second wife, whom he married in 1933, nine years after the death of Myriam's mother, Elisabeth. Marianne was Myriam's step-mother in her formative teenage years and during the war when the family fled to England. Albert and Marianne were divorced in 1947.

"There must have been 12 or 15 people, and they were mostly gay," said Thomas. "We were all sitting on the floor and drinking wine and someone brought out the marijuana and started to roll joints. And Marianne said, 'You know this is so quaint that you Americans are rolling your own cigarettes,' and Myriam said, 'Oh no, mother, this is marijuana.' And Marianne goes,' Oh my God!'

"So they were passing this joint around and of course Marianne joined in. We smoked three or four and she never let it pass. And she said, 'You know, this really doesn't have any effect on me. I'm quite tired. I'm going to bed.' We all said goodnight and she went off to bed. She was staying in the little chateau. About half an hour later she came back down and said, 'I am *so* hungry!' Myriam fixed her a tray of cheese and lettuce and tomatoes."

Hartley said Robert worried about Myriam's open-door policy, a Statue of Libertine welcoming any and all.

"I think they quarreled about her activities—smoking dope, hanging out with gay men, liking hippies, and so on. Maybe Robert worried about having someone screwing an underage boy in the house. It was courting danger to have people who were 16 in your house.

"Robert probably felt sorry that Myriam had been condemned to rustication in the provinces, and that he had to let her have a certain latitude to have friends and do things. Myriam didn't see any reason why people who were 16 shouldn't have a glass of wine or smoke a joint."

Chuck didn't look much older than 16. Before learning how he had met Myriam through Thomas, McGarrell "just assumed he was one of the young people who drifted in."

Unlike those who drifted in for a while to sample the scene then split, Chuck kept coming back to Myriam. Not to smoke dope. He could do that anywhere. Nor for sex. Neither was interested. Their relationship was deeply rooted in trauma, in deep-seated need. Chuck's for someone to exorcise his gay shame, Myriam's for a son to replace the one she lost.

"Chuck was like a son to her," Davezac said. "He was two things, a son and a young man. His attention would flatter Myriam. You know, she's coquettish in certain ways. She said, 'Oh, Shehira, he was telling me about his life, he was telling me this and this...' and I said, 'Myriam, you are out of your mind. Don't be an idiot! There could be bigger things for you—professor at Indiana.' She said no, he's like a boy, he's like my son.' This was the real thing with her about Chuck. It wasn't about drugs, it wasn't about any of these things, it was her feeling about children and not having one."

McGarrell scoffed at what she considered Freudian overreach. "There's a big difference between 'son she never had' and 'pet.' The house was always full of young people, including neighborhood children and various students who became, along with the cats, surrogate children."

But only one would become locked with her in a fatal embrace. Chuck invited one of his closest student-friends at BHS to accompany him once to meet Myriam.

"He took me to her house," she said. "It was just the three of us in a smallish room, a bedroom, I think. We got high. She was like Mrs. Robinson to me. I think she was a little jealous of the two of us. There was something about her that he thought was really great. I didn't like anything about her. I didn't like the place. I just didn't have a good feeling at all. There was just something very dark about her, very dark."

Hello, Goodbye

*T*he first two weeks of January 1968 the No. 1 song on Billboard's Hot 100 list, which Chuck posted religiously on his classroom bulletin board amid images of pop stars and newspaper headlines about the Vietnam War, was "Hello, Goodbye."

He was so attuned to the Beatles, his psyche tattooed with their words and music, it's hard to imagine Chuck would have missed the bittersweet synchronicity of the moment: Saying hello to a new year and semester at the same time he was starting his long goodbye to BHS and Bloomington. Unlike the Beatles, his plans were not bulletin board material.

It's likely that only his family knew he visited California over Christmas break and returned with a job for the fall. Or so he told Sally and, later, a few confidantes. He divulged no details of his move to administrators, even in the resignation letter he would later submit.

It was common in such letters to give a reason for leaving, like taking a job elsewhere or a spouse being transferred, and to offer words of appreciation, even if pro forma, such as: "I would like to say that I am very proud to have been a member of the faculty of the Bloomington Metropolitan Schools."

Chuck's name-rank-serial-number letter, dated March 15, 1968, included no perfunctory niceties.

"I am now in my second year of employment with the Bloomington Met system. This year ends in June. I do not plan to return for the following school year. Very truly yours [signed], Charles Ancil Walls III."

The school board accepted Chuck's resignation at its meeting on April 4, 1968, the day Martin Luther King was murdered in Memphis.

Just six weeks later, *The Optimist* offered a radically different version in a story about departing teachers. It ran under the headline "French, English, German Teachers Leaving," with a subhead, "Students Say Farewell." The two paragraphs about Chuck included a summary of his work as teacher and *Optimist* advisor, highlighting some of the innovations which had roiled old-school sensibilities.

"In Mr. Walls' two years at BHS he has introduced many new concepts to the English department. Having sophomores write a term paper on the novels *1984* and *Brave New World* was Mr. Walls' idea. Other than novels, Mr. Walls' classes study poetry through the lyrics of Paul Simon, Bob Dylan and John Lennon. In this way they learn the poetic nature of today's music, themes, and symbolism. His students also study Liverpool poets of today. He has also expanded the scope of *The Optimist* to include a literary section of music and book reviews and columns."

All of that was undeniably true, if not admired by colleagues with a death grip on the past. The concluding sentence, on the other hand, was of dubious accuracy. "He will be leaving for Cambridge, Massachusetts, in September to attend the Experienced Teacher Fellowship Program at Harvard and will be returning in August of 1969."

The idea of Chuck escaping to Harvard then *returning* to BHS ran counter to what anyone had been told, and to common sense. As far as Sally knew, Chuck was going to California and never coming back—a happy outcome for all involved. Maybe the Harvard scenario was a remnant of his one-time hope to move east closer to Gail, his fellow chaperone and platonic lover at Oxford, Sally surmised.

But that doesn't explain why Chuck would tell his family that he was California-bound and, at the same time, approve an *Optimist* story stating flatly that he was headed the opposite direction. Maybe he was "just keeping all options open since I know he didn't trust BHS not to blackmail him out of a better job," Sally said.

If *The Optimist* story was wrong about Chuck's destination, it was not a reporting error. "I didn't make anything up," said Lee Ann Watson, a sophomore journalism student who wrote the story. "It was exactly what he told me. I did not have him for English and wouldn't have known anything about *1984* or *Brave New World*."

Chuck introduced another element to *The Optimist* more subversive than haiku and movie reviews: Artful sarcasm directed at the BHS powers-that-be. So artful it apparently sailed high over their flattops. Case in point, Kent Harvey's mordant dismay over broken air-conditioning units in windowless classrooms, which he said threatened the "well-being and perhaps even the existence" of students.

"Intellectual stagnation can be neglected as not directly related to the goals of the school," he wrote acidly, "but simultaneous physical discomfort cannot and must not be tolerated. We urge the student body to exhibit a real social consciousness by speaking out on this crucial issue."

Harvey's satirical mission had nothing to do with getting the AC fixed. Suffocating classroom conditions were a metaphor for administration efforts to stifle expression of social conscience and to stop the venting of opinions on any issues more "crucial" than temperature control.

In the winter and spring of '68 this was becoming a fool's errand for school administrators. Authority everywhere was fighting a doomed rearguard action against history. A long-gathering storm with howling winds of change from a thousand directions was making landfall across America. The response of BHS officials was to shutter the windows and cover their ears.

In January the illusion of "victory" in Vietnam, nurtured by President Johnson and his generals, was shattered by the Tet Offensive and Viet Cong assault on Saigon. CBS anchor Walter Cronkite visited Vietnam in February and told viewers the war could not be won. Forty-five Americans a day were dying there. In March, U.S. troops murdered 450 women and children at My Lai. BHS administrators invited a State Department official to defend U.S. policy to history students.

Protests against the war and the draft were erupting everywhere. Students at Columbia University occupied administration buildings. At IU there was a peace fair in Dunn Meadow. Young people—cannon fodder for LBJ's war—joined the presidential campaigns of Eugene McCarthy and Robert Kennedy. Both visited Bloomington during the Indiana primary campaign and filled the IU Auditorium to overflowing. BHS refused to grant excused absences to students who attended the Kennedy speech.

In a letter printed in *The Optimist,* student Ann Shere said the decision was "totally reprehensible and contrary to the alleged goals of school" to prepare students for their future role as citizens. "By placing those who did go to the speech in the category of truants, the administration deprived their charges of a unique opportunity to view civics and practical politics in action."

The administration did make a small concession to Shere and other "truants" who dared to broaden their educations. It did not suspend them from school as it had students who wore black armbands to protest Crane Navel Ammunition Depot.

Shere's letter was as close as *The Optimist* got to editorializing on Vietnam. But under Chuck's guidance it did provide solid reporting all around the issue: three full pages on the Indiana primary including coverage of candidate speeches, examination of their positions on an "honorable negotiated settlement" in Vietnam, and results of a straw poll that showed teachers favoring McCarthy and students Kennedy. Richard Nixon was the second choice of both groups.

As he had all year, Chuck made ample room for book, movie and record reviews. Sara Zylman wrote about *The Fixer*, a Bernard Malamud novel. Harvey gave a rave review to Bob Dylan's *John Wesley Harding* under the headline "Return of the Master." He made sure there was a feature on Simon and Garfunkel when they came to town in late February for two concerts. Chuck took Sally, rescuing her from the family home in Sullivan which she regarded as the seventh circle of boredom.

The Graduate opened at the Von Lee Theater earlier in the month. Tickets were $1.50. Chuck offered extra credit to students who saw the movie.

"I remember his obsession with *The Graduate*," said Pruett. "I know he saw it many, many times. I saw him at the theater the night I went. I was from the west side. We didn't go to movies. That was an expensive proposition. I'm sure I went because of that [extra credit]."

The only person in Chuck's world more desperate to get out of town, figuratively crossing off the days on the wall of his jail cell called Bloomington High, was Harvey. The family had moved from Ann Arbor, MI, in 1966 when William Harvey was named dean of the IU law school.

"He intensely hated Bloomington and especially BHS," said Veronica Sebeok, a classmate and one-time girlfriend. He sloughed off Bloomington as "crappy and horrible." Whippet thin, straight brown hair swept to the side, a sly smile belying a serpent's-tooth wit, Harvey recalled a young William F. Buckley. He and Chuck became close friends and, in their final hours at BHS, co-conspirators in a valedictory roast in *The Optimist* of the demons who had tormented them.

Debate team. Standing, from left: Mark Brickell, Kent Harvey, Julia Wrubel, Andy Mahler, Diana Liu, Scott Lloyd, Jim Warden. Seated: Kevin Craig, Frank Qualls, Jan Griffin, Phil Schrodt. [*Gothic*, 1968]

Published in May only weeks before graduation, Harvey's withering 1,000-word broadside was disguised as encomium and ran under the headline "Student Thanks Administrators, Faculty for Aid." No takedown of a school's hierarchy could get into the school newspaper without help from someone inside—someone looking to even the score before moving on.

The words are Harvey's but in them you hear Chuck's plaintive, angry, weary voice:

"I would like to extend my appreciation to many of the teachers I was fortunate enough to have, and to a number I was fortunate enough not to have. They worked tirelessly to shape me into the sort of person they knew I should be. It was through their ingenuity that I learned that every problem has one solution, every question has one answer, every argument one side and that color is really an illusion since the world must properly be seen in black and white...

"Next I must turn to those administrative officials who managed with a minimum of effort (always a minimum of effort, please) to pave the high school path with carpet tacks of dogma and creaky 19th century educational philosophy. I have to thank the administration for conscientious efforts to keep me, and my classmates, pure in thought, word and deed by offering helpful suggestions on appropriate wearing apparel, hair styles and skirt lengths...

"If perhaps at times I have been somewhat antagonistic and wild-eyed, have tried to rock the boat, even occasionally forgotten that school is not a place for individual thought, it is also a time to offer my apologies. I was young then. It was only a phase, and I believe I have grown out of it now, seen the light, if you will...

"There are a few minor changes I would like to see made at BHS, but they are the concerns of future classes now. And after all, if there is one lesson that I have learned at BHS, now that I am old and world-wizened, it is that you have to patiently wait for change, and wait, and wait, and wait..."

Hail Caesar! The Fairy Fetcher

C huck made no secret of his preference for students in his own image: literary-minded, hyper-verbal, hip to pop culture, unafraid to test, even breach, established norms in the name of intellectual inquiry and artistic endeavor. He called them "alpha" students.

Tony Solomito was none of those things. He sat in the back of Chuck's sophomore English class, rarely speaking, neither participating nor disrupting, a smiling face in the crowd of more garrulous classmates. A classic "beta" student in Chuck's hierarchy.

Heidi, alpha daughter of iconic IU humanities professor, Henry Remak, said Tony was "just another guy in our class—quiet, good-looking. It was a fairly small class, but Tony stayed pretty much in the background. He just didn't have a personality that had him up front and looking for attention."

Most of the time. There were exceptions. One was whenever Tony was behind the wheel of a go-cart at a local dirt track where "up front" is exactly where he wanted to end each race. Another one, not by choice, was the day he was drafted to play Julius Caesar in a classroom production of Brutus assassinating Caesar. A yearbook photo captured the climactic moment.

A group of girls in makeshift togas and tin-foil helmets and armor look on with stifled giggles as a Brutus in khakis and button-down shirt thrusts an imaginary dagger. Tony, sporting a cardboard laurel wreath, leans away in horror, smiling like a hyena. The caption reads: "Julius Caesar, really Tony Solomito, dies laughing when Brutus [Richard Johnson] assassinates him in Mr. Walls' English class."

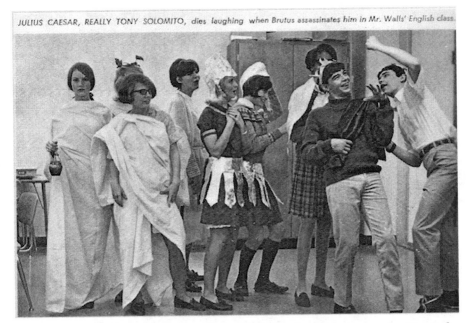

JULIUS CAESAR, REALLY TONY SOLOMITO, dies laughing when Brutus assassinates him in Mr. Walls' English class.

Caesar, Tony Solomito and Brutus, Richard Johnson in classroom production. Left:
Heidi Remak and Pam Lawrence [*Gothic*, 1968]

"That was embarrassing because I always just hid in the corner," Tony said. "I was really shy, except at the race track. I could go piss behind a light pole right in front of 2,000 people and not think about it. It was the only place I was ever comfortable."

It was a puzzling casting choice. What caused Chuck to single out a beta student with stage fright to play Caesar? Tony brought only one obvious attribute to the role, but it was the same one which regularly secured lead roles in Hollywood.

"Tony Solomito was gorgeous," said local prosecutor Tom Berry, who came to know Tony. "He may be the handsomest lad I've ever seen."

Doe-eyed with olive skin and flawless features, Tony jumps out from the sea of awkward-stage sophomores in the yearbook as a precocious dreamboat. A heartland Sal Mineo. "A little stud," band director Traub called Tony, who played sax in the varsity band. "You couldn't ask for a nicer young man—just an outstanding young man in school."

The golden apple did not fall far from the tree. Tony's father, Joe, was a strikingly handsome man, a fact noted in newspaper stories—and there were many over the years documenting his escapades.

"My dad was originally in the stone business but got busted for tax evasion and went up for six months," Tony said. "They were digging up money in the sandbox when I was a little kid."

That much is true but hardly does justice to a picaresque career which made Joe (also described as "dapper" and 'burly") a larger-than-life, technicolor character in a community of Ma and Pa Kettle farmers and pallid ivory-tower academics.

"He was a hustler," said Carp Combs, who grew up in the sticks outside Bloomington where Joe operated. "I know him from an oil scam he ran in Polk Township around Chapel Hill. There's a marginal oil field down there that's produced maybe 20,000 barrels total since, like, 1920. Joe got investors to open it up again in the early-mid '60s. They lost tons. He walked. Then he was involved in very marginal real estate developments. He sold a subdivision, laid out with roads that were graded but not paved, fire hydrants in. Problem was, the fire hydrants were just sitting there, not hooked up to anything because there were no water lines."

In 1957, a federal court jury convicted Solomito of dodging $54,000 in income taxes. Solomito testified he received $130,000 in cash "gifts" from (unnamed) friends and family, which he thought were tax-exempt, and buried it in a basement drain for safekeeping while serving overseas in World War II. An IRS agent said Solomito told him he was "carrying watermelons for a living while his widowed mother was mortgaging property and borrowing money" to get by at the same time the drain supposedly was choked with cash.

After the trial, to verify his bizarre claim of burying cash and to put some unearthed dough in the bank to pay overdue taxes and fines, Solomito and his wife led journalists and law enforcement officials on a tour of Solomito Savings and Loan. The Courier-Journal (Louisville, Kentucky) put the story on the front page.

"Solomito and his petite wife took the group first to a bedroom closet where they removed clothing to reveal a safe. Solomito spun a combination and removed packets of currency totaling $10,180. Removing a section of wallboard from the closet wall, he exposed a smaller safe from which he took an additional $10,000.

"Moving to his backyard, Solomito broke through turf, dug down two feet, and removed a mortar-cast object, which he broke open to reveal a Mason jar. It contained $10,000 in bills, wrapped in tin foil and a plastic sack.

"While opening concealed safes and digging in the ground for hidden dollars, Solomito steadfastly maintained that he is innocent of willful evasion. He acknowledged, however, that concealing his sizable fortune in his home 'might make anybody who doesn't know me think the whole thing is fantastic.'

"I want this to be a warning to anybody else not to try to operate their businesses and their homes from a cash box. Regardless of where the money came from, nobody is going to believe you."

Tony was born in 1953 at Bloomington Hospital three blocks from the Joe Solomito Stone Company, one of a cluster of companies where limestone extracted from local quarries was milled and fabricated. Solomito and others like him were models for the stonecutter dad, Ray Stoller, in *Breaking Away*. The summer of '68, Solomito ran a used car lot at the same spot in Bloomington where fictional Ray Stoller hustled buyers ("Refund? *Refund!?*") in the movie 10 years later.

Like young Dave Stoller, the movie's protagonist, Tony helped his dad at the lot, washing cars and even selling a few. He also bought his first car, even though he was 15 and had only a learner's permit to drive. "A Triumph Spitfire come in with low mileage, a '66 in great shape. I paid $600 for it."

Solomito sold the stone company in 1955 and the family moved to a farm northwest of town. It was a Huck Finn boyhood for Tony, exploring the hills and hollows and woods of untamed Monroe County, crawling through caves, skinny dippin' in the clear-running creeks. At 7, he was shooting guns and racing go-carts. On the farm he trimmed fruit trees, fed the cows, mended fences. He began smoking cigarettes at 14.

"I was sitting on a bank fishing and the guy next to me didn't have mosquitoes around him. I did. So I grabbed one of his cigarettes and it kept mosquitoes off me. One of my biggest regrets is that I ever started smoking."

His best buddy and partner in teenage foolishness was Steve McClung, who lived a mile away. In the summer of '68 they were 15 and couldn't legally drink or drive, which proved no obstacle to their adventuring. Tony's mother drove them to town each morning for driver education class, and no teenager worth his salt ever has to go beer-less.

"We could always go down to Kirkwood and find someone to buy beer for us," McClung said. "We'd take it down into the valley. Tony's house set up on a hill. You could walk out his back door down through a field where they kept cows and then into the woods, and the woods dropped down into a valley, a beautiful area. The kids called it Beer Can Alley. There was a gravel road that went down across a creek and up the other side and came out onto Acuff Road. We'd drink beer down there in that hollow, camp out, and go to drivers ed class in the morning hung over."

It's difficult to imagine two places and cultures in Bloomington so near yet so far apart as the IU opera department and Beer Can Alley. They came together when Rod Mortensen, an opera student from California, volunteered with Tony's scout troop. He'd been an Eagle Scout growing up and, at 24, already had served a tour in the army when he arrived at IU to study opera stage direction.

Ron Mortensen

Tony Solomito

Steve McClung

Scout leader Rod Mortensen with scouts Tony and Steve [Courtesy of Rod Mortensen] and [*Gothic* 1968]

One day a paint store worker with a comic strip name, Buzz Hawk, told Mortensen about the scout troop he led. Mortensen, who missed scouting, was intrigued.

"In those days high school kids were Explorers. He had an Explorer post that was an Indian dance team. Now, I obviously knew a thing or two about lighting and makeup and all that sort of thing. And I knew a thing or two about scouting. So I went out one time to see what they were doing. And these kids were good. They could put on a real show. He asked for my help. I said, yeah, I can."

After a time, Hawk got busy with other projects and Mortensen agreed to take over as leader. There were about a dozen boys in the troop at any given time in the 18 months Mortensen was in charge. Tony and Steve were two of his favorites.

Tony was "an outgoing kid, friendly, dedicated to what he was doing, and willing to learn. And he just had a lot of fun. He was the All-American boy," Mortensen said. "Most of the boys met that description, some more than others, but Tony was up there at the top of the line. And Steve was the same way. They were cut of the same cloth. Just good, solid kids."

Post 100 was sponsored by the local Optimist Club which had a day camp south of town with a concrete block building equipped with running water, restrooms, and heat, and a big open floor ideal for rehearsing.

"What they were doing was not an easy thing to do," said Mortensen. "It takes time and practice and you've got to be good at it or it just doesn't go. They made their own costumes, rather extensive costumes. Those that knew worked with those that didn't know until everybody knew. It was a group effort.

"We went around to a lot of Cub packs and service clubs. Anyone who wanted us to do something, we were there. If a supermarket had a grand opening our guys would dance in the parking lot as part of the event. We'd try to set it up so we were going camping the next weekend and we'd get all the groceries free from the supermarket. It was great to go in and say, 'Okay, we need five of those and six of these.'"

Mortensen enforced a straight-and-narrow ethic on alcohol and drugs, especially marijuana which grew wild in the sticks.

"In Army I had seen people getting very badly screwed up with drugs. I don't know that I ever talked to them as a group about it. There wasn't any standing up and preaching. But I let them know that's not part of the game. That would have been the kiss of death and they all knew it. I was not going to have any kind of garbage like that going on. They didn't drink or smoke, they didn't raise hell beyond having a good time."

It was different when the Indian dancers were off the Mortensen reservation. Tony and McClung partied under the noses of Tony's parents.

"We had this great big barn and we partied there," Tony said. "We'd get malt liquor off my older sister and drink it till we puked. My parents were okay with it as long as we weren't out on the roads or driving or anything else. They were pretty cool that way. Marijuana was the devil to them."

It was Tony who introduced him to weed, McClung said. "We would get high in his bedroom. It was unbelievable how naive his parents were at the time. How in the world could they have not smelled it? How could they have not smelled us in the morning?"

In school, Tony was drifting—an early poster boy for dazed and confused.

"My whole high school experience sucked. I was a year younger than most people in the same grade. I was never cool enough to be a hippie. The first thing that happened to me at BHS, a guy was talking to me about dancing with his girlfriend. Next thing I know I'm thrown up against the wall. Another guy said to him, 'Better be careful if you ever piss off that little Italian.'"

Tony was wary of his assigned school counselor. "He said come to my house, this is my address, drop by. No way I was going to do that. One of my best friends, I was kidding with him and said, 'You know I attract gays.' Then one time we were at this restaurant and a guy came over and propositioned me. After that my friend always called me a 'fairy fetcher.'"

During the school year Tony didn't think about Chuck's sexuality. Unlike the counselor, Chuck never gave him any reason to. He thought Chuck was a good teacher but wasted on him. "I was unteachable at the time." One assignment that did bring Tony out of his fetal position in the back row was analyzing rock lyrics.

"Every once in a while I'd talk about something, and I could tell he didn't want me to say that the song was talkin' about drugs."

Not after all Chuck had been through that year—suspension, new rules emasculating him as a teacher, being fired in all but name. He was gun-shy about classroom discussion of drugs. Another scandal on his way out of town was the last thing Chuck needed.

What Chuck *wanted*, in spite of his better judgment and best laid plans, was quite another matter.

"At the end of the school year we met one time," Tony said. "He had a little smoke, you know, so we smoked some. After school was out we just kinda ran into each other. We'd go out and smoke and talk about this or that, and every once in a while he might move his hand over, and I'd be like, no. It made me feel uncomfortable but it wasn't malicious. He had the hots for me. I was so naive that I didn't realize what was going on."

Avoiding the Grey Twilight

*K*ent Harvey's majestic indictment of the establishment which Chuck ushered into *The Optimist* just weeks before graduation would not be the last time Chuck's spirit dumped cold water on the self-satisfied pretensions and ceremonies of school authority.

His parting shot was delivered by surrogate at commencement for the BHS Class of '68 held at the Indiana University Auditorium in June. Chuck had no hand in writing valedictorian Julia Wrubel's commencement address. But her contrarian message, skewering her own classmates, echoed the tone of a commentary Chuck wrote for *The Optimist* when the Class of '68 were juniors.

In the aftermath of class elections in September 1966, he praised the Class of '69 for "an admirable lack of apathy," lauding the 18 sophomores who ran and lost. He cited Theodore Roosevelt's dictum that it is "far better to dare mighty things...than to take rank with those spirits who neither enjoy much nor suffer much because they live in the grey twilight that knows not victory nor defeat."

Chuck meant the Class of '68 which he noted had offered many fewer candidates for office. He was politely scornful of their reasons for not showing up on the ballot.

He wrote, "More than one junior explained they were not seeking office because they had no apparent chance of winning what they felt amounted to a popularity contest. It may conceivably be true that some class elections are popularity contests, and while voters may not always elect the best man, it still is nice to see the best men running. Next September we can only hope the Class of '69 will, as juniors, have more candidates than did the Class of '68. Avoid the grey twilight."

Wrubel, daughter of an IU astronomy professor and a book editor, possessed a daunting intellect and quiet nose-to-grindstone work ethic which seemingly gained her immunity from front office harassment, even when she fished for it. She was in the small group of students who wore those black arm bands protesting the Crane Naval Depot.

"I remember other people being called into [principal] Jones' office. I was walking around, like, 'Pull me in! Pull me!' And they wouldn't. I thought, 'What's wrong? How come I can't get arrested?' I mean, boys were being pulled in for *haircuts*."

Administrators clearly felt commencement was in safe hands with Wrubel giving the main address, following talks by three other outstanding graduates. To ensure nothing untoward tarnished the august occasion, organizers dictated the speech topic: "What has BHS done for us?"

"We had to hand in our speech in advance and rehearse it at a practice commencement," Wrubel said. "I had prepared a stupid speech like everybody else, how BHS prepared us for the future and all that. When I got home after practice I thought, 'This is horrible, I'm not going to say this.' So on the morning of commencement I sat down, put the *Messiah* on the turntable, put on the headphones, and wrote something like, 'Ask not what BHS did for us, but what we did for BHS.'

"I talked about all the changes, all the things we had done. I forget what they all were, but they were momentous because this was 1968 and we were transitioning. We were becoming outspoken, we were changing the dress code, we were challenging hair length, we were doing all kinds of other things, and we were leaving this as our legacy to upcoming classes.

"I didn't think it was subversive. The audience didn't boo, they applauded. But it hadn't been approved by sponsors of the commencement, and they were not happy. There was talk of revoking my diploma."

Wrubel's grave transgression was injecting a scintilla of context and truth in her remarks. The *Herald-Telephone* reported: "Miss Wrubel chided her classmates for their few material contributions to BHS but explained they had served as a transition class between the old BHS and the BHS of tomorrow."

Some classmates were offended by the idea they belonged to a do-nothing class. The appalled elders were hoping that Wrubel's address would mimic the string of timeless platitudes in Jones' farewell message to the Class of 1968 published in *The Optimist*. It was a message that could just as easily have been addressed to the Class of 1868.

"I suspect many of you feel that it has been a long and arduous journey. Hopefully you have developed a desire to learn and some insight into how to learn and to solve problems, problems which do not presently exist. Take some time to reflect, reassess the past years, but keep one eye on the road ahead, for there is much work to be done. Set new goals for yourself..."

After doing everything in his power to make BHS a fortress against the future by freezing dress codes, banning free speech in *The Optimist* and punishing social activism, it was predictable that Jones had absolutely nothing of relevance to say to the Class of '68.

The notion that each high school class is special and distinct from all others, as different from one another as the planets, is a cherished sentimental fantasy. One class may indeed be blessed with superior athletes who bring championships. Others by a wealth of National Merit Scholars, a musical prodigy, a future statesman, a poet laureate, a Nobel scientist or humanitarian. Or none of the above. It's all the luck of the demographic draw and redistricting.

The only thing that truly separates classes, defines each one and tells its story, is the calendar. The Class of '68 began its senior year in the afterglow of the Summer of Love and was ending it amid political tumult, assassination, race riots, blood in the streets of America and in the villages of Vietnam. Few classes had ever been so sucker-punched by history.

The 423 graduates, their family and friends gathered at the IU Auditorium on June 2, nearly two months to the day that Martin Luther King was murdered on a motel balcony in Memphis, three days before Robert Kennedy was gunned down in a hotel kitchen in Los Angeles. "CONG DEEP INSIDE SAIGON" blared a banner headline in the Indianapolis Star. The No. 1 song in America was "Mrs. Robinson," an ode to lost innocence.

Wrubel's jab at her classmates was not the only tiny rebellion. Deppe, author of the fraudulent petition that saved Chuck's job, crossed the stage barefoot. A female student who shared joints with Chuck said, "We all talked about what we were going to do or say when we were handed our diploma. I took mine and said, 'Marijuana!'"

The *enfant terrible* of the day just wanted to get out of town. "I grabbed my diploma and ran!" Wrubel said. "All the way to New Mexico for the summer."

One high school tradition Chuck honored and took quite seriously was end-of-year signing of yearbooks which he treated as a literary exercise. He avoided the breezy, impersonal pap that was the staple of yearbook inscriptions: "It's been a joy having you in class. Good luck!"

His were customized for each student like postcards of their time together. Sentimental, poetic, often bittersweet, sometimes inscrutable, always deeply felt.

They are not long, the weeping and the laughter,
love and desire and hate;
I think they have no portion in us after
we pass the gate..
They are not long, the days of wine & roses;
Out of a misty dream
Our path emerges for awhile, then closes
Within a dream.
    —ERNEST DAWSON
    'ACROSS the FIELDS of YESTERDAY'
    (Vitae Summa Brevis)

Two worlds we have lived together, and when
I miss you I will remember pieces of both — trying
to get you to see 'Taming of the Shrew', going to the
Paris. discothèque, learning from Bob Cotterall,
looking for Mary Harkness, the boat ride from Dover,
running around Stratford, taking a picture of you on
a rock in Stonehenge.

    Most of our painless times came then. But we
did accomplish some things this year. And we
learned from and with each other. And I do
believe we made a difference. .
    I will miss you.
                        Chuck Ubells

[Peggy Pruett's *Gothic* 1968]

They are not long, the weeping and the laughter,
Love and desire and hate;
I think they have no portion in us after
We pass the gate.

They are not long, the days of wine & roses;
Out of a misty dream
Our path emerges for a while, then closes
Within a dream.

Ernest Dowson's VITAE SUMMA B[reptor]
'Across the Fields of Yesterday'

Gothics each May make me realize how differ[ent]
our lives were patterned a year earlier. Nine month[s]
have contained so much that is good and bad. Learnin[g]
to learn is a mysterious, fascinating process. The express[ion]
on your face when suddenly you perceived something new
many times made me realize why I have wanted to be wher[e]
I have been. I will miss many people next year
but will 'find strength in what remains behind...'

Mr Wall[s]

Heidi,
I would have never
made it through health
without you your just the
... .but, words can't explain.
.. all the advice dool
Krottzgh

Heidi just one
fine. Surely
individual I know to have
... HK

[Heidi Remak's *Gothic* 1968]

- 174 -

Sweet Lorraine

looking for a sunshine summer

Words often are trite groping attempts to identify
feelings of moods, memories, and mystic communication.
I will run the risk of seeming sentimental: you have added
to the intensity of my consciousness through such exuberance
as displayed on the PSYCHE staphe (who says abortion is illegal)
This has been a year of extremes. In the future, ...?...,
I will have a photograph to preserve your memory...

Chuck Walls

[Veronica Sebeok's *Gothic* 1968]

Clockwise: Cathy Hoff, Nancy Barr, Jana Kellar [*Gothic* 1967, 1968]

"I remember going into his room at the end of the year, rather nervous at the prospect of asking him to sign my yearbook," said Mary Johnson, who had Chuck for sophomore English that year. "He was ready for me with quotes he'd selected from Phil Ochs, Marty Balin and Country Joe and the Fish. Who knows if they were intended specifically for me, but he was ready."

In Johnson's yearbook Chuck wrote: "We talked of magic and mystic qualities during the year. Several times it happened as a spark caught between several minds. Learning can be of a spiritual nature. Watching it happen to you and Eric and Heidi and the others who were true 'images of innocence' was one of the high points of my life."

Chuck's inscriptions often took up most of a page. Above his message to Heidi Remak, he quoted all of Ernest Dowson's elegiac poem "The Days of Wine and Roses" in his slanting, left-handed cursive.

"*Gothics* each May make me realize how different our lives were patterned a year earlier. Nine months have contained so much that is good and bad. Learning to learn is a mysterious, fascinating process. The expression on your face when suddenly you perceived something new many times made me realize why I have wanted to be where I have been. I will miss many people next year but will find strength in what remains behind."

He preceded his message to Pam Lawrence, a sophomore, with a passage from Wordsworth that was longer than his inscription, and concluded with a cryptic reference to a classmate that left her baffled.

"Words run the risk of seeming trite in a yearbook and seldom can recapture all the magic of a year such as this," Chuck wrote. "I think there is an air of permanency to what has happened in our class. You've added so much to it. I will miss you next year, but will see you someday according to Kay."

He meant a friend, Kay Terry, Lawrence said. "I'm not sure why she was predicting he and I would see each other 'someday.' It was probably some silly joke in class. But he remembered to include it. Wish I could remember, but I can't."

Nancy Barr, *Optimist* news editor her senior year, was not a fan of Chuck's leadership style, nor his inscription in her yearbook. She said she never wanted or asked for it. Chuck must have signed it when *Gothics* were being passed around the room, she said.

"We've gone through a great deal together," Chuck wrote. "Some bad times were educational. And I'll always remember your fantastic scrapbooks. People aside, it was a very good year, and your organization helped getting it out most of the time on time. Do you recall that glorious September morning when we emerged from Mr. Vondy's room in good spirits? But that was many years ago. Goodbye."

Barr was baffled by mention of things that never happened, names she didn't know. "'Bad times were educational'? My scrapbooks I never showed him, I'm sure. Mr. 'Vondy'? Many years ago? Goodbye? Was this deep or crazy?"

With Chuck, sometimes both. Veronica Sebeok, daughter of two professors of semiotics, experts in decoding signs and symbols in language, could have used their help deciphering Chuck's inscription. "You have added to the intensity of my consciousness through such exuberance as displayed on the Psyche strophe (who says abortion is illegal?). This has been a year of extremes. In the future...? I will have a photograph to preserve your memory."

Psyche strophe? Abortion? "I doubtless did not know what he meant at the time," Sebeok said, "but dared not ask given my drive to assure I wouldn't be suspected of not being cool enough, a juvenile motivation for much of my behavior."

To a junior girl of conservative bent, an *Optimist* staffer with whom he had little in common, Chuck wrote in concrete, affectionate terms: "We're very different in many ways, and yet have gotten along marvelously. That will remain one of the nicest aspects of this school year to me, as will the experience of learning to know you. You seem to have changed since September. I think you've kept your optimism and exuberance but have grown more aware of the shape that the world and its smaller components are in. Your seemingly unlimited pep adds much life to the two periods we are together. You could be the saving force next year. I'll be watching."

Then there was Peggy Pruett. She and Chuck shared a lot of history in two years. He was her chaperone for the summer in Oxford. Pruett was feature editor and an ally when Chuck gave *The Optimist* its own Prague Spring. She never had Chuck for English, to her keen disappointment, but he invited her to read one of her poems in his class—a singular moment for someone admittedly "not a free spirit."

"Two worlds we have lived together," Chuck inscribed, "and when I miss you I will remember pieces of both. Trying to get you to see *Taming of the Shrew*, going to the Paris discotheque, looking for Mary Harkness, the boat ride from Dover, running around Stratford, taking a picture of you at Stonehenge. Most of our painless times came then. But we did accomplish some things this year. And we learned from and with each other. And I do believe we made a difference. I will miss you."

Wrubel was never a student of Chuck's but was drawn into his orbit by the lively conversation and laughter she heard coming from his classroom. Her senior year she was a guest teacher in his *Optimist* class. Sara Zylman, a student in the class, wrote in Wrubel's yearbook: "It's been great getting to have you as guest teacher. Good luck next year when you're running free. Remember me from 8:25 to 3:15 locked in this prison."

Chuck's farewell inscription to Wrubel began with lines from Paul Simon: "Seasons change with the scenery, weaving time in a tapestry..." At the end, he borrowed from Grace Slick: "You'll be inside my mind on future days of splendor. Can you imagine us years from today?"

Later in the summer, as he prepared to leave for California, or maybe Harvard, Chuck wrote to Wrubel in New Mexico.

"I think our fair city has finally recovered from your hippie speech, regained its composure and relaxed with the comfort of knowing that all's right with the world. It was a valiant deed, though, which in all seriousness I admire you for. Futility hardly makes an action meaningless; sometimes that very quality adds to its precious aspect, as with the *1984* analogy of the mother shielding her child with her arms from bullets."

It was the highest praise Chuck could bestow: She had avoided the grey twilight.

Room 101

*L*ike most college towns, Bloomington empties out in summer, losing half its population in an exodus of students as sudden as the swallows vanishing in a cloud from Capistrano. Drained of its economic lifeblood and wellspring of vitality, the town grows listless. The pulse slows. A hazy torpor descends. The time and temperature sign at a bank on Kirkwood seems frozen at 88 degrees, marking a state of suspended animation.

"July 16, 1968—Nothing of consequence has (or ever) happened here," Kent Harvey said in a letter to Julia Wrubel in New Mexico. He was spending the summer in *Les Miserables* mode painting houses to pick up extra cash before leaving in August to enroll at the University of Michigan.

"I've been hearing terrible reports about all the things going on over at BHS during the summer session," Harvey wrote with cold glee. "Apparently they are very glad to be rid of us, but still feeling stung about the callous way in which we reacted to their great interest in our mental well-being. References are particularly common to your subversive commencement address and that horrible, satirical, sarcastic article in the great school newspaper (monitors the throbbing pulse of school life, you know)."

Chuck, patron saint of Wrubel's commencement address and midwife to Harvey's evisceration of his BHS jailers, was taking a graduate class in Old English lit at IU. After surviving a near career-ending scandal, he seemed buoyant and energized by his imminent departure for a new job and hipper pastures in California (unless it was Harvard as he told *The Optimist*).

A typed letter to Wrubel on July 24, 1968, less than three weeks before his family was to drive him west, bubbled with the curiosity and catholic interests of the pop-cult renaissance man who transfixed students at BHS.

Chuck wrote: "After class I went over to Jim Sutton's house, at the moment free of parents who are vacationing in Michigan while he goes to summer school. He has the new Cream LP and Laura Nyro's 'Eli and the 13th Confession,' lyric content of which we debated. Both are tremendous albums. A new Doors LP arrived yesterday. No 11-minute song as on their other two, but words to 'The Celebration of the Lizard,' a theatre composition by Morrison as yet unrecorded, and 'The Unknown Soldier,' plus other head-spinning performances like 'Five to One' and 'Love Street' and two cuts musing on joys in summer and winter.

"I then stopped by Cathy Hoff's and had a nice rapping session, ranging from *LIFE's* review of Hermann Hesse and its fascinating cover article on Young American Nomads Abroad, which you should read, to the *New Republic's* observation that it probably doesn't matter who's elected president since the right-wing trend will apparently elect a do-nothing Congress.

"*LIFE* has indignant replies to its 'New Rock' 40-page article on Airplane-Doors-Hendrix-Cream, including a piece by Mother Frank Zappa, which brought nostalgic tears to my stomach. Aforementioned replies include BHS-type gems like 'Whatever happened to Dick Tracy and Babe Ruth' and 'Can you pick one selection with a tune pretty enough to whistle?' Wow.

"After visiting with Cathy I went to pick up three records I'd lent Corry and Mark and wound up rapping for an hour with Dr. & Mrs. Rieger, who are really a groove. He lent me three of his favorite books totaling 2100 pp. to read. I should isolate myself for the coming year if only to catch up on all of that.

"For you to contemplate: Is *Rosemary's Baby* a religious film, a grotesque allegory appropriate to the very world of hate, negativism, and violence which we generally if reluctantly accept? Does it represent the forces apparently so much in control today? And if the plot level is excruciating, how disturbing is the thought that it might as well happen, given world events as they are? Its climax is a parody of classic theological pronouncements.

"Did you see the Xerox Bill Cosby special—'Lost, Stolen or Strayed'? I hadn't realized *Birth of a Nation* was so gross a film, depicting the KKK as saint/savior. I got a classic reply to my letter on gun control from [Congressman] John T. Myers saying he was carefully considering alternative gun legislation 'more attractive to those of us who prefer not to become carried away by emotions.' Isn't it reassuring to have such a conscientious man looking after our interests?

"This is my parents' address; I'm staying with them and saving my funds for September. I don't know what my address will be then but mail can be forwarded from here. I'll be here until Aug. 10."

Rev. Walls had been transferred in June from the Methodist Church in Sullivan to the pulpit in Bedford, 25 miles south of Bloomington in the limestone belt. After the school year, Chuck moved home to economize. Rent at Cascades Apartments was $125. Maudlin, who held the lease, said he always paid the full rent then waited and waited to be reimbursed $62.50. "Chuck was very hard to get money out of," he said.

They had met and become friends as undergrads. One year Ray was governor and Chuck vice-governor of Shea House at Foster Quad. As roommates they got along despite warring views on Vietnam, Chuck's tight fist and Maudlin's habit of leaving lights on. "It drove him crazy," said Sally, Chuck's sister. Ray teased Chuck about his habit of making a list every night on an index card of the things he was going to accomplish the next day.

Chuck never smoked dope in front of him, Maudlin said, and he had no reason to be suspicious of a package that arrived for his roommate one day. "It was about a foot square, two inches high, and very light. Chuck said it was two shirts he ordered from Chicago. I believed him. I was so naive. Just a dumb kid, the son of a dirt farmer from Logansport [Indiana]."

The roomies employed a traditional technique to signal when they had an overnight guest: a knotted tie hung outside on the front door knob. Chuck used it once, Maudlin recalled, but he never glimpsed the guest. He saw visitors other times, boys and girls he assumed were students, but they stayed in the living room. Maudlin had no clue Chuck was gay.

Tony had just an inkling from Chuck's awkward, tentative advances when they met up near the end of the school year and smoked some weed. As summer set in with drivers ed and Indian dancing gigs with the scouts, Tony tried to close the Chuck chapter of his life, referencing an Orwellian nightmare learned in his class.

"We had talked about 'Room 101.' It was a *1984* thing where everybody told the truth. I told Chuck if I ever said 'Room 101' that it means 'stay away.' We kept talking over and over that I didn't want to see him anymore. I didn't want to be called by him anymore. I didn't want anything anymore. Room 101."

Chuck was not to be denied. Still burning behind the index-card facade of propriety was the compulsion which had driven him to engage in risky behavior that would have ended in his firing, if not for the loyalty of students who lied for him. The hubris of escaping led Chuck to believe he could dodge the bullet a second time. Even as his promised land, California, beckoned on the horizon, obsession led him to Beer Can Alley.

"He started coming by my house and calling me," Tony said. "We owned property beside Beer Can Alley and he came down there and gave me a bag of grass. I don't even know why I took it but I did. I just got all screwed up, stopped racing. I was just enjoying getting high, drinking, experimenting with it."

Chuck's bag of bait worked.

"The relationship ended up progressing some," Tony said. "A lot of times we'd go over to Myriam Champigny's house. They had a circle of friends and they'd be there smoking dope and hash. I was never very good at socializing. I really liked Myriam, and her friends all seemed nice, except the gay issue kept coming up. Like if somebody wasn't gay they weren't cool.

"Myriam showed me where the gun was in the house. I brought up guns, that I liked to shoot, so she showed me. When I was 7, I had a .22 automatic for plinking, and I knew if I ever did anything wrong with it, my dad would never let me touch a gun again. Chuck was the complete opposite. Guns terrified him. Every time anyone said anything about a gun he was like, 'I don't want to touch one.'"

Sometime before Chuck moved to Bedford for the summer, Tony visited his apartment. Chuck gave him a sandwich "laced with something that knocked me out," Tony said.

"I don't know what it was, I have no idea. I know there was a hallucinogenic effect to it. He was in the process of trying oral sex on me when I woke up. It was humiliating. My pants were down. His roommate came in, and I took off. I was too young to have a car so I ran into Cascades Creek and watched his blue Camaro going up and down the road. He was looking for me."

Flashing a sideways grin, he added, "If it had been a female teacher I probably wouldn't have minded."

The book-sharing, idea-swapping Chuck who dropped by friends' homes for high-spirited rap sessions was not the one Donnadee Blair encountered when she returned to Bloomington after chaperoning students on a summer trip to Mexico.

"When I got back, rumor was circulating that Chuck Walls is in a drug-related, crazy social situation. By that time I would say I was no longer a confidante of his. I felt he had made his decision and crossed into wherever he was, and I had no interest. He was the one who called and wanted to get together.

"He came over and we had chili that I fixed with my group of friends. We sat outside on the porch. One of those great big huge limestone porches. He didn't mix with anybody else. The two of us had a chance to talk. But he didn't share anything with me. Nothing. We ended up talking about going back to school. I felt like Chuck was almost a lost soul."

This was the Chuck who included in his letter to Wrubel the lyrics to South African jazz artist Hugh Masekela's dark protest song "Coincidence" with this chorus:

"I hear the laughter of the cannons/as the soldiers are dying/and a million children burning /from the fires of hating/cause the world ain't ready yet/for all the babies on the way."

Chuck decided, in the midst of his infatuation, that it would be a good idea to introduce Sally to Tony.

"Chuck really thought a lot of Tony and wanted me to meet him. He was going to take me to Bloomington to meet him. I wasn't dating or anything like that, but Chuck said he was a really creative kid and he thought really good things were going to happen for him. He said, 'I think you two have like minds.'

"So he set up this meeting. But I got very sick very suddenly, a strep-throat kind of thing. My mother said, 'I'm going to have to get you to the doctor, you can't go.' The second Chuck walked out the door to meet him [Tony], my illness suddenly stopped. The illness kept me from being able to go and there was not another opportunity. I was just not supposed to meet him."

On July 3, a month after Sirhan Sirhan murdered Robert Kennedy with a handgun and around the time Myriam showed Tony the gun in their home, the *Herald-Telephone* published a timely letter to the editor.

"To the gun lovers or defenders whose line of reasoning is, 'It is not the gun, it is the man behind it,' I call their attention to the article in the *Herald-Telephone* entitled 'Stray Bullet Kills Brown County Man.' The article made page 1 in our local newspaper. But was this death announced over the national television and radio networks? Did it make front-page news all over the country?

"No, because the Brown County man was not well known, he was not a public figure. When we use such adjectives as tragic, senseless, shocking and unbelievable in connection with the killing of a well-known figure, let us remember it also applies to those who do not make headlines. To Shirley Anderson the 'Brown County Man' was well-known. He was her husband. To Celeste he was well-known too. He was her father. And to Mrs. Bionne he was also well-known. He was her son.

"I have never met Everett Anderson, but I think his death is tragic, senseless, shocking and unbelievable. The article said two teenagers, about 14 years old, were target shooting with a .22 caliber rifle. In this case will anyone dare to say it is not the gun, it is the man behind it? This was just two children playing, which precisely proves my point. A totally accidental killing of this kind shows the need for gun control and strong firearms legislation even more than does the planned murder of a public figure."

It was signed...Mrs. Robert Champigny.

Conscience of a Conservative

*T*homas Hoadley, who made headlines across the state and triggered reefer paranoia in Bloomington with the 1963 arrest of an IU student, was as Hoosier as the limestone from local quarries which brought his family great wealth and greased his path to election as Monroe County prosecutor.

His successor, Tom Berry, was an Ohio kid who attended IU Law School as a last resort and had no desire to stay. "I wasn't very impressed by Indiana as a state," he said. Berry came from a long line of Buckeyes. He was born in Columbus and graduated from Ohio State University.

"I wanted to be a lawyer and go to the OSU law school. They said okay, you're in. But you're an out-of-state student. Now wait a minute. My grandfather was in the first class ever to graduate from OSU in vocational agriculture. My father graduated there in the same thing. True, they said, but your parents moved to Indianapolis two years ago. Your fees will be doubled. I did not have the money."

Berry moved to Indiana where he paid in-state fees and started on a path that made him the accidental prosecutor. After graduating from IU Law in 1965, he landed a job at the firm where he had interned as a student. When Berry complained about the pay, his boss, Jim Ferguson, used the old-boy network to line up a part-time job for him with Hoadley.

"Next thing I knew, after I'd been out of law school for two months, I was deputy prosecuting attorney in Bloomington city court. Which was perfect because every day I tried cases, and I tried them with 10 minutes preparation," Berry said. "You really learn to think fast. I was a pretty good trial lawyer. I was on the moot court team at IU Law. I could say words pretty well. So I knew that whatever I did it would be saying words in a courtroom as opposed to writing words in a brief."

In Indiana then, all prosecuting attorneys, chiefs and deputies, were part-time. It was customary for prosecutors to have private practices on the side. In the Republican primary in spring 1966, Hoadley won nomination to run for another term in November. In August, he withdrew from the race and said he was moving to Florida after his term expired in January.

Republicans greeted the news with mixed feelings. On the one hand, Hoadley had become a cartoonish figure in his Captain Queeg-like pursuit of socialists on the IU campus who, he claimed, were plotting the violent overthrow of the state government. His pot bust of IU student Nancy Dillingham in 1963 when she was scooped up in his tuna-net trawling for Commies, added to the Hoadley follies.

On the other hand, despite his buffoonery Hoadley was a likely winner in November. With just two months before the election, Monroe County Republicans were left with no candidate on the ballot.

"So they looked around, and here I am," Berry said. "I am just a kid. I'm not from Indiana. I know nobody. They said, 'You're going to be our candidate.' And I said, 'Ain't no way I'm gonna be nominated.' They said, 'You don't understand the process. Precinct committeemen vote so it doesn't matter what the world thinks, all that matters are 66 township committeemen. All you have to do is go meet 'em.'

"Well, if you saw my picture, I looked good, and my wife was gorgeous. She was fine with it. It was a wonderful opportunity. Not only the pay hike but the prestige. It would help my practice, would do everything good for me. So all of a sudden this kid is the prosecutorial candidate, and I had no idea what to do.

Tom Berry, candidate for prosecutor 1966 [Courtesy of Tom Berry]

"Ferguson said, 'Buy 10,000 pencils and just stand in the shopping center and hand them out to everyone who comes by.' It was a bit odd to have this kid stop you and say, 'Hi, I'm Tom Berry, I'm running for prosecutor, have a pencil.' It was a pretty good gimmick.

"Still, I'm completely unknown, I can meet only a very small number of people. We didn't know it at the time, but in 1966 Republicans couldn't lose. It was a landslide in Monroe County. All the Republicans won. I was dead last. But I was in."

When Berry took office in 1967, the stable of white, middle-age, square men who ran the city were becoming aware of the dimensions of the drug "problem" in Bloomington. Over the next two years the city would spend "more money, time and effort to stem the flow and use of narcotics than any period in its history," the *Herald-Telephone* reported. Police had the names of dozens of suspected users and pushers, but they were outnumbered. 'We must realize we have a very small department of 46 active policemen who have to perform a variety of services in this community which has a metropolitan population in excess of 65,000 and a vehicle population that exceeds 40,000," said Mayor John Hooker.

Berry brought to the job the standard biases of someone whose wonder years were spent in a small midwestern town. His dad's work took the family to Bowling Green in northwest Ohio where Berry graduated from high school in 1957.

"I was always politically aware, even in high school. I was a Goldwater Republican. I could quote you *Conscience of a Conservative*. Mom was a mild Republican, my father was a mild Democrat. Neither of them ever talked about it. There was no religion in our home. I never got a lecture on religion."

Or drugs. In the late '50s, young Berry was more likely to run into Marilyn Monroe than a drug dealer on the streets of Bowling Green.

"I don't think by the time I graduated, there ever was a marijuana cigarette in Bowling Green. I never heard of it until I was in a fraternity at Ohio State and had a roommate who was hooked on marijuana. It seemed exotic and scared me and I never tried it. But he was one of my best friends, a charming guy, one of the best trumpet players in Ohio. He finally went with the Stan Kenton band.

"No one ever sat me down and said marijuana would send you to hell, but I decided it would probably be dangerous, it might lead to something worse. Of course I knew it was illegal. The narcotics guys were always following my roommate. They would sit down and chat with him."

Berry, who liked to say, "Although I was often wrong, I was never in doubt," had no doubt he could handle a job he had never done, even if it was the highest-profile job in Bloomington after mayor. He was 27 when he was sworn in.

"I had a big enough ego that I thought I can do this by learning on the job. But I was also realistic enough to know I hadn't a clue what I was doing. I had an office in the courthouse, about 200 square feet on the third floor. I had a deputy, I had a secretary, and we ran the thing sort of out of our hip pocket. One of the ways we did it was we could fill out warrants that had been pre-signed by a judge. We had a stack of 'em.

"It was unusual. Everyone did it. And it was unusual because it directly violated the Constitution, which requires you to go before a judge or magistrate. It had been done that way in Indiana for a hundred years. I didn't even think about the fact it was illegal. I'm not even sure I knew it was illegal. I just knew this was the way it was done."

As deputy prosecutor in city court, which processed misdemeanors, Berry handled DUIs but no drug cases because all marijuana charges were felonies. Many of the cases coming across his desk involved IU students.

"We had a lot of incidental stuff. Casual use, possession of small amounts, and every time it came to my attention I had a felony on my hands. They carried horrendous penalties. If the kid was clean otherwise, they usually got a suspended sentence. But it's a suspended felony, on their record forever. There is no expungement in Indiana. You're a felon. It follows you like a dark cloud."

Berry had a high success rate in the courtroom. He had fallen into a role that suited his chromatic personality, his gift for saying words, and rakish good looks—Burt Reynolds minus the mustache. "Tom was a very dramatic arguer, very flamboyant," said his deputy, Randy Bridges. "He was fun to watch." Berry would not disagree. "I was really good. I mean, I really was."

On one issue Berry was a bitter disappointment to the morality police on the hard right. At a time when the porn flick *Deep Throat,* starring Linda Lovelace, was being banned at theaters across America, Berry let it run for a year at the Cinema West Drive-In, nicknamed "Smut West," outside Bloomington.

"People would drive down the road and there she is doing her thing. I had delegations coming in and saying, 'That theater is showing *Deep Throat* and let me tell you what it is. It's a violation of the pornography act'—which it was—'and we want you to prosecute the owner of the theater!' I just said no. I'm up to my hips in serious criminals and I don't think I was elected to be the county censor. And I'm just not going to do it."

Berry's libertarian leanings and sympathies did not yet extend to marijuana. He was elected to arrest and lock up users and sellers of weed.

"I may have winked at it when I was at OSU and my roommate was involved, but I'd come to believe that marijuana was dangerous, a much greater threat than alcohol. A gateway drug. About two marijuana cigarettes and you're mainlining heroin. So I had no problem with the law. After I became prosecutor, I gave a speech to a service club in which I said we've got to stop the scourge of marijuana."

Berry's attitude would evolve and soften over time.

"It became obvious as I got more experience that I was dealing with two classes of criminals. You have the Carlisle Briscoes" [a KKK sympathizer who torched a book store run by black IU students] "and a whole lot of people like him, vicious people that attacked folks, who really just ought to be shot.

"And then you had a different class of people who were smoking marijuana. In almost every situation, very nice people, not like Carlisle Briscoe or a hundred other people I could name. And at some point, I decided I just didn't want to file felonies anymore over incidental marijuana."

That time did not come soon enough for Chuck Walls. Or Myriam Champigny.

A Hard Rain's a-Gonna Fall

*A*fter his rude awakening from Chuck's psychedelic sandwich and fleeing to the woods of Cascades Park with Chuck in hot pursuit, Tony was desperate to be rid of his relentless suitor.

"Any time he'd call I'd say, 'I'm being watched, leave me alone.'"

Chuck's August departure for California was fast approaching. Tony figured he could lay low and elude Chuck until he left town. Ironically, the plan was subverted by the most wholesome part of Tony's summer—his involvement with the Explorer scouts. Indian dancing, spelunking, rappelling, scuba diving, camping. Troop leader Rod Mortensen "was a really cool guy," Tony said.

"I was 24, young enough to sit down and talk with the guys and laugh and carry on and have a good time and we did," Mortensen said. "I think maybe they would talk in front of me and say things they might not have in front of someone who was a little bit older."

Tony and McClung made the mistake one day of getting too comfortable around their scoutmaster. The troops had come together for war-gaming or bushwhacking or other Katzenjammer Kid fun in which Mortensen always was an eager player.

"He wasn't the guy you went to for a merit badge in rowing," Tony said. "We all thought we were going to Vietnam anyway." (He drew a high draft lottery number and dodged those bullets. So did McClung.)

"I think it was a Saturday afternoon we were out at the camp," Mortensen said. "They were sitting around and started talking about these people they were hanging out with, about smoking dope and all that sort of stuff. I was taken aback and said so.

"They weren't just talking about weed, they were talking about mushrooms and psilocybin, all kinds of stuff. When I found out who their source of supply was, it really rattled my socks—adults who were in a position of trust. The only name I remember is Gloria. And there was the guy who was the English teacher."

Not wanting to "make a federal case out of it in front of the whole bunch," Mortensen pulled the boys aside. "They came clean, gave me the story."

McClung said he was questioned first, without Tony in the room.

"He grilled me about it, told me how this is hurting Tony, that I was his best friend and if I cared about him I would come clean," McClung said. "Then he had me in the room when he confronted Tony. I was afraid Tony was going to be mad at me for spillin' the beans to Rod. I remember looking at Tony and saying, 'He said it was hurting you.'"

Mortensen said, "I told them, 'Look, we need to talk to your folks.' They asked if I would go with them, and I said sure. They were afraid."

Mortensen paid separate visits to the boys' homes. "Both sets of parents were pretty calm, cool and collected about this. They were disappointed in the kids but there wasn't any screaming. I think the boys were afraid there would be and that's one of the reasons they wanted me there. There was a realization amongst everybody that this had to stop.

"It was changing times and all that, but no one knew what the hell was going on with that stuff. They just didn't. It was all by guess and by gosh. These were two good, solid kids, doing well in school, a lot of things going well for them, and this guy was providing them with stuff in contravention to any common sense. He could have screwed up either of those kids so badly."

Alarm rippled through the extended families. Mortensen went to the home of Steve's sister and his brother-in-law, Ted Scott, where the boys often hung out and spent the night. Scott, an intense Navy vet with no love for the hippie culture, was incensed by what he heard. A consensus formed that the matter must be taken to the police.

Tony was ready. "Chuck just kept calling me up. Except now my parents were next to me when I was talking. I basically told him '101,' our code, which obviously he didn't pay any attention to. I figured the only way out of it was to get him busted."

In the early days of August, Mortensen, Scott, the boys, and their fathers met with the Criminal Investigations Branch (CIB) at Bloomington Police headquarters downtown. Questioning was conducted by Chief Detective Russell Parks. In a confidential report, with Tony's name redacted because he was a minor, Parks detailed his meeting with Tony and his father.

"I questioned Tony in the presence of his father reference [sic] his relationship to Charles A. Walls, an ex-school teacher at BHS, and a lady by the name of Mrs. Myriam Champigny. He stated he had been to the residence at 1040 East Maxwell on occasions and had been furnished marijuana by Mrs. Champigny. Also he had been furnished marijuana by Charles Walls, 23 years old. Walls had dispensed him marijuana at the Commons on the IU campus, and he had a bag of marijuana and a pipe which Walls and Mrs. Champigny had furnished. They were going to have a going away party for Mr. Walls on Friday night, August 9, as Mr. Walls was leaving to go to school at Harvard University, and that he would help in setting up either a buy or some arrangement where we could arrest the two of these people while the party was going on and that there would probably be other people present. Probably young teenagers like himself."

Detective Thomas Simes also questioned Tony, who detailed the beginnings of his relationship with Chuck.

"He states that in the early part of May, as he was acting rather tired in class, Mr. Walls asked him if he would like to turn on. There had been discussion among the children [students] before this and Tony went with Mr. Walls to his apt. at 1945 N. College and Mr. Walls showed him how to turn on and gave him the marijuana to turn on with. He turned on several times after this with Mr. Walls in the same apt. After one of their conversations Mr. Walls asked him if he would like to meet a lady and took him to 1040 E. Maxwell Lane where he met Myriam Champigny.

"At this residence he turned on with Mr. Walls and Mrs. Champigny two times. He states that Champigny has marijuana in various parts of the house but he doesn't think her husband knows anything about it. He further states they have other types of narcotics at the house also, and that Mr. Walls carried marijuana between the seats of his car. He states that Mrs. Champigny plans to go to Portugal soon and that Mr. Walls is leaving Tuesday (Aug. 13) for a year's fellowship at Harvard."

Police questioned McClung about Tony's sexuality. "They asked me if I ever had any indication he was gay. I said no, Tony liked girls. I guess that's the first thing adults think when an adult and a young teenager are involved. They couldn't fathom the thought that maybe Chuck was just genuinely interested in nurturing young minds. All Tony ever talked about was they had great conversations and got stoned together."

Tony, the acclaimed "fairy fetcher," laughed off the idea he was gay. "I slept in a barn with Steve for years, got drunk, and we never did anything. I guarantee you."

Chuck already was on the Bloomington PD's radar when the boys divulged their stories about him. "This name came to light last winter along these same lines," Parks noted, alluding to Chuck's suspension after parents of a student found diary entries about parties where he smoked dope.

Tony was pressured to provide names of BHS students he thought or heard were using marijuana, and those he suspected or were rumored to be pushers. The police seemed eager to expand their list, however speculative. Tony gave only names, but the confidential file, 13 users, 6 pushers, had personal data presumably gathered by police.

Among the users:

"Jim Sutton- 18 (approx) - Acid head, speed Freak. 1214 E. First. I.U. Student, WMA. 5-10, 150 lbs, Blk Hair, Dk complected."

"Name redacted - 16. Speed, Grass. Address unknown. BHS student. WFA. 5-4, 125 lbs, Blnd/Brn Hair, Lt complected. Has been known to pass speed caps."

"Name redacted - 17 (approx) - Acid, Speed, Grass, etc. Address unknown - BHS Student- WMA. 6-0, 155 lbs, Brn Hair, Medium Complected. Spent last summer in Berkley, Calif.

The suspected pushers included an 18-year-old white male who played in a local band. "Currently employed as a salesman for a music store across from the Juke Box. May have quit pushing."

A white female BHS graduate who "will probably attend a small college in S. Indiana. She intends to make her way pushing." The report includes her "code name."

"Chuck Walls - 24. Grass. lives in Bedford/father - WMA. 5-9 1/2, 145 lbs, Brn Hair, Lt complected. For the past two years has taught English at B.H.S. Has distributed marijuana (not sold to students)."

"Miriam Champienge (last name probably incorrect spelling) - 40. Acid, Sylo, Grass. 5-0, 120 lbs, Brn Hair, Medium Complected. Currently holds high office in the Monroe County Humane Society. Has connection with the top area suppliers of illicit drugs. Presently raising marijuana in her backyard. Husband (I.U. Professor) is not aware of her drug activities."

By the afternoon of August 7, police investigators decided the incriminating material they had gathered about Chuck and Myriam had reached critical mass. It was time to go to the prosecutor. Parks arranged a meeting at the CIB with Tony and his dad, Berry, Lt. Simes, and himself.

Berry was keenly aware of the six F.B.I. agents J. Edgar Hoover had posted in Bloomington to hunt for communists plotting to overthrow the government. "They were on my back to help fight it." Hoover also hated drugs.

"If ever there was a little drug deal, this was it," Berry said. "But I didn't appreciate that at the time. I was 29 years old, tremendously naive. I believed marijuana had the potential to destroy our country as we knew it. These people were evil and it was my job to stamp out evilness. I was a Goldwater Republican, I was a zealot, this case walked in the door. It had everything."

The going-away party for Chuck at the Champigny home on August 9 was the focal point of planning at the CIB meeting.

"After discussion as to how to conduct the best legal search, seizure and arrest, it was decided that a search warrant would have to be drawn up to be used at the party," Park wrote in his report. "It was decided that an agent or investigator from the prosecutor's office be driven by the Champigny home to get a better picture of the layout to draw up a search warrant. Tony was to go along with the consent of his father."

Playing stool pigeon was repugnant to Tony. "Even though I was mad at Chuck, it still wasn't right. I didn't want to do what I did." He had no choice. "I was going to be convicted of something if I didn't cooperate."

"It was just blackmail by law enforcement," Berry said. "The cops said either you say words, true words, or we bust you, too. It was made clear to Tony that nothing would happen to him unless he decided to cross them. If he did he would be charged in juvenile court and I would probably ask to have it transferred to adult court."

Lt. Simes, an investigator from Berry's office, Tony and Joe Solomito headed out on their reconnaissance mission. Cruising by the Champigny home they saw Chuck's blue Camaro parked outside. They dropped Tony off and sent him inside "to see what he could come up with, maybe get some more marijuana or another buy from them," Parks said.

What he found instead were Chuck, Myriam, and a few of her friends insistent on conducting a "truth session" with him, Tony said.

"It was all about whether I was gay or not. It was just like they couldn't believe I wasn't gay. We started smoking dope and hash. I saw a Polaroid camera laying there and I just started taking pictures of everybody. It just kept going on and on, 'You're gay. No, I'm *not* gay.'

"It was frustrating to me because I didn't feel like I looked gay or acted gay or anything else, and I just couldn't believe they didn't understand that I tried to give them a way out so many times. 'Room 101.' I thought I'd made it clear that when I talked about Room 101 it was danger. You know, bad."

Shortly after 5 o'clock Wednesday afternoon, Parks received an urgent call at home from Lt. Simes. He told Parks that Tony had called his father from Myriam's to say the Friday party for Chuck had been cancelled. If there was going to be a bust, Tony said, the police needed to move *now*.

Berry was notified. An affidavit was hurriedly drafted charging Myriam and Chuck with possession of marijuana. Parks signed the affidavit, warrants were issued, bond was set at $1,000 each. A seven-man raiding party set out to stem the scourge of marijuana on Maxwell Lane.

Let It Be

*A*round 5 o'clock Wednesday afternoon Bruno and Maureen Civitico stopped by the Champigny home. They had become friends with Myriam and Robert through the McGarrells. "Bruno was one of my husband's most beloved students. A beautiful hugely gifted painter," said Anne McGarrell. The Civiticos were preparing to leave town after completing their graduate work and needed a place to store bookcases while they were in Italy.

When they pulled into the driveway, a blue Camaro was blocking access to the garage where they hoped to store the cases. After the "truth session," which failed to bump Tony off the straight and narrow, he and Chuck had repaired to the back bedroom where they were smoking copious amounts of weed and hash. Chuck came out to move his car, then returned to the bedroom.

"We had maybe met Charles, as Myriam referred to him, once before that day," Maureen said. "I don't think so, but it could be. In the summer, Myriam always had her home and garden open to artists, writers, poets. She was exotic to me and being around her open, warm, intellectual atmosphere was intoxicating. All the students loved her."

It took nearly an hour for the Civiticos, with Myriam's help, to haul the bookcase shelves up into the rafters of the garage. As was often the case, Robert was out of town, in California teaching a class.

Shortly after 6 p.m., "We were standing in the kitchen with Myriam after storing the bookcases," Maureen said. "We were chatting, saying our goodbyes and thanking her for having been such a good friend to us while we were in grad school."

Suddenly, without a knock on the door, police officers burst in the door from the carport brandishing arrest warrants. Other members of the raiding party rushed in through a back door leading to the garden. Startled cats scattered in all directions. Not seeing Tony or Chuck in the living area, Chief of Detectives Russell Parks went to the back bedroom.

There he found Tony sitting on the bed talking with Chuck. The record player was going. Chuck had "a very stupor [sic] expression on his face," the detective noted later in his written report. "I identified myself after he [Chuck] asked me if I was a member of the family."

Elsewhere in the house, Detective Harold Aynes encountered the Civiticos, non-suspects who nevertheless were fleeing toward the exits. In his report Aynes described what happened when he entered through the carport door.

"I observed a man later identified as Bruno Civitico. He jumped up and started to go out the west side of this room. This would lead out into a garden-like place. A female subject came out of the kitchen and started to leave by the same door. I got Bruno stopped but this woman later identified as Maureen Civitico got outside before I got her stopped. She and Bruno both returned to the house with me."

That's when Aynes spotted Myriam coming out of the kitchen. He recognized her from the description in the arrest warrant.

"Are you Myriam Champigny?"

She replied with a single word: "Yes."

Aynes read the warrant aloud and advised Myriam she was under arrest.

By this time, other officers had arrested Chuck and put him in their cruiser, handcuffed in the back seat. "Bruno went out and talked with him," Maureen said. "Offered him a cigarette and some words of support while the police searched the house."

The search yielded a smorgasbord of cannabis treats and paraphernalia, detailed in Parks' report.

"We found one jar full of seeds which appear to be the same as marijuana seeds. We found plastic bags in two different drawers with a green leafy substance which appears to be marijuana. We found a glass with several cigarette butts, some homemade and hand-rolled that are known as roaches. These are suspected to contain marijuana. We also found a pipe with tin foil in the bowl which Tony (redacted) said Walls had just recently smoked before we arrived, and we suspect that the residue in this pipe to be marijuana. We also found a broken-stemmed white clay pipe with residue in the bowl which will be tested for marijuana."

In her recollection of the bust years later, Maureen mentioned an additional police discovery not listed in case reports: bricks of compressed weed, a common method used by dealers for transporting and storing marijuana.

"I don't believe for a minute that the bricks of marijuana the police photographed in her kitchen cabinets were hers [Myriam's]," Maureen said. "Interestingly, they were placed right where the coffee mugs were kept."

Shehira Davezac, who phoned Robert in California with news of the bust because Myriam was too traumatized to do it, voiced a theory popular among Myriam's closest friends.

"Somebody planted it in the cupboard. I think Chuck at the last minute got frightened and planted it. Myriam said to me, 'Shehira, could you imagine if I had it, that I would have it right in front when you open the cupboard?' I very much definitely sense that she had been sold down the road."

At trial Myriam's attorney would claim that Chuck brought marijuana to the house in a silver ice bucket in which Shirley Walls routinely packed a lunch for Chuck on days he traveled to IU for his graduate classes. Tony showed police a compartment in the ceiling where he said Myriam hid weed, but it was empty that day.

But weed was still spilling out of cupboards a week after the bust, according to a statement Myriam wrote out on IU Department of French and Italian stationery and gave police, noting the exact date and time she penned it: August 16, 8:30 a.m. She sounds thoroughly mystified by the sudden appearance in her home of a substance that *might* be pot.

"I, Myriam Champigny, being in my kitchen with my friend Maureen Civitico, fixing our breakfast and starting to feed the cats, opened one of the kitchen cabinets where I usually keep my dry cat food and saw a crumpled paper bag which did not look familiar. I touched it and felt it contained something soft. Maureen, being right there, saw me open it and inside were two plastic bags filled with what looked like dried herb. Until I talk to a lawyer I think it best to record this finding, which I feel has some connection with the charges against me."

Davezac dismissed as silly Tony's insistence that Myriam was growing marijuana in her backyard. But Tony knew weed when he saw it. He planted some himself out in the country. He marveled at Myriam's exquisite display. "It was pretty artistic how it was planted along the little walk there. You could swear it was just some flowers growing." The police didn't collect a sample, he said, because "the pot in her garden wasn't bloomed out then."

Another piece of evidence gathered at the scene and used in court but not itemized in police reports were photos, party snaps Tony took that day with the Polaroid he found lying around. One photo showed Chuck holding a pipe wrapped in tin foil. "It wasn't my camera, it was just there. I just started taking pictures of everybody."

Also confiscated were random items and knick-knacks that were not used as evidence in court and eventually returned to the Champignys:

Goblet with dried roses
Canister with dried flowers
Paperback copy of *The Book of Grass*
Cellophane pack of dried substance (unknown)
Pasteboard round box with "Puss n Boots" story.
Two Dramamine tablets
Opened pack of radish seeds

At the time of the bust, there were people in the house besides the Civiticos, said Tony, but they were not arrested. Nor was their presence noted in the police report. "I think one of them turned state's evidence to keep anything off of his record, and that's how come he ended up being a judge," Tony said.

In interviews with us, Tony declined to name the judge. "Room 101," he smiled nervously.

In the final act of the charade to save his skin, Tony did the same perp walk away from the house as Chuck and Myriam.

"When they were loading me in the back of the police car, Myriam came over and said, 'Don't worry. It's going to be okay.' I was arrested but I wasn't really arrested. They handcuffed me and took me in and I had to do everything, but I wasn't really arrested."

Having held up his end of the deal, Tony was released to his parents at the station. A detective warned Tony not to believe anything he heard or read about the case.

After signing statements acknowledging their rights to remain silent and to have an attorney present for questioning, Chuck and Myriam were photographed, fingerprinted and taken to the Monroe County jail, pending release on $1,000 bail.

Chuck volunteered to give a statement. It was a rambling, inarticulate discourse you might expect from someone who had spent the afternoon smoking dope. In it he tries and fails, at times laughably, to portray himself as a babe in the drug-infested woods of Bloomington.

Police: "Since you have been arrested for possession of marijuana, would you give us info as to where you have obtained marijuana."

"I can give you information pertaining to person and place from which marijuana can be bought. I was made aware of this place, although at the time not knowing it was this type of place, by a stranger who befriended me in The Other Side record shop. This person introduced himself after several days of casual conversation as 'New York.' He said this was the name he went by. He seems to be around 19 years old, very scruffy-looking, about 5 feet, 8 inches tall. He wore blue jeans with a big rip in the thighs. He took the initiative in making the acquaintance with me, discussing music, IU sports, etc.

"Finally one afternoon he approached me at The Other Side and said he thought I might like to meet a friend of his. I said alright. He took me to a house containing apartments and introduced me to the occupant named Mark. Several people were there and none of them were introduced to me. They were playing music and drinking Cokes, talking and laughing. I stayed for about one hour, talked about records with some of them then left. Mark extended an invitation to me to return, which I accepted but did not intend to actually use. About two weeks later the same New York—again at The Other Side—invited me to return there. Fairly reluctantly, I did so. Mark was exceedingly friendly and warm and again invited me to return. After several more weeks, on the spur of the moment, I did so.

"Thereafter at various intervals I would return for usually half hour at a time to sit and talk. On those occasions people would use words such as 'pot, grass, lid, scoring, pushing,' but were not doing anything. Over a period of several visits I became more aware of their affirmative attitude toward these things. On one occasion a stranger entered and Mark asked him to 'Front me some bread for a big deal.' The stranger gave him several dollars. Other times Mark would refer to being on the verge of big deals, of shipments from Chicago, of a contact at the music school at IU. On one visit I asked for a cup of coffee and he told me I would have to fix it because he was 'too stoned.'

"One time during the winter, I was at Nick's English Hut and Mark was there and invited me for that evening. He said we have something going I think you will like better than this. The apartment was filled with people, about seven, none of whom I knew beside Mark. He took a pipe from one and handed it to me and told me to take a deep puff. He told me to inhale deeply and hold it as long as I could, and he had me do this repeatedly over two hours. After several rounds he asked me how I felt and I said my lungs were a little hot but that is all. Before the evening was over he said, 'This is boo, man.' I said what? He said, 'grass, pot, mary jane.' He asked how I liked it and I said I couldn't tell anything.

"At a future visit he offered me some more and I didn't take any, but on the third occasion I did. Repeatedly after that, on some but not all occasions, I would find his apartment filled with people looking college age and they would be smoking and hand the pipe to me. During the summer I went there several times and he has given me several packages of what apparently was marijuana. He did not charge me for this and said he could afford to give it to some of his friends."

Police: "Did you in turn give it to any of your friends?"

"No. There was someone at the record shop who asked me if I wanted to buy some, he said that he had some. I said that I didn't really need to buy any."

In his summary report, Lt. Simes said Chuck "would evade direct questions and would lie about others. Therefore the statement was terminated and I advised him that if he decided or wanted to tell the truth to come back tomorrow at 2 p.m."

A day which began in keen anticipation of his departure for California ended with Chuck posting bail and heading home in darkness to Bedford. He was dreading what tomorrow would bring.

A Day In the Life

*M*idnight was nearing as Chuck pulled his Camaro into the driveway of his parents' limestone ranch home on Sycamore Drive in Bedford. No one inside knew that only hours before he had been arrested on felony drug charges. Radio stations hadn't picked up the story yet and afternoon papers would not have it till the next day.

Chuck's late arrival that night was no particular cause for alarm.

"His hours were erratic but that didn't seem unusual considering all he had to do," said Sally. "Chuck had been studying for an Old English final at IU as well as getting ready for his upcoming move. He would come home and eat—Mom saved dinner for him—then study."

For Sally the countdown to California was a melancholy passage. Chuck's departure was leaving an unfillable void in her universe. Stifled by a childhood spent in small Indiana towns, Sally treasured time with her sophisticated older brother. He was her tutor in the pop arts, revealing the poetry in rock lyrics, taking her to concerts in Bloomington, introducing her to literature like *Lord of the Flies* and *Brave New World* that she was not likely to encounter in Bedford schools.

"I needed a recent picture with my brother who would soon be living thousands of miles away. My mother had shown me a photo of Chuck in a black Beatles-style turtleneck. When I saw it, I knew I had to have mine taken with him in that shirt. Each day I waited for him to see when

Sally Walls, 1972

we could fit in taking the picture. Days passed and he would always say 'tomorrow.'

"When he came home late Wednesday he was in a bad mood. I thought it was because he had the final. He was curt with me when I asked again. He said it was too late but we could take it in the morning before he headed out. I was determined to be ready Thursday morning for my chance."

Chuck was up most of the night. What fresh hell awaited him the next day? What was to be done? Sally got up to use the bathroom but saw a light under the door and went back to bed. Shirley later found Chuck burning papers and photos in the bathroom sink. He was upset that she asked what he was doing.

Thursday morning, Sally overslept but awoke in time to hear Chuck preparing to leave. She threw on some clothes and rushed out as he was walking to his car.

"In a hurry, he called back to me: 'Tonight, Sally! Be ready and I promise we will do it when I get home.' He got in the car, rolled the window down and smiled at me. I guess he realized how little time he'd had for me lately. 'See you tonight!' I waved and watched him drive out of sight.

"Wherever he was going, he didn't tell Mom and Dad. Later we found a note where he wrote, 'I want so much to tell Sally, but I'm concerned she'll feel she has to tell mom and dad, and I don't want to put her in that position while I'm figuring this out.'"

Sally assumed Chuck was headed for his final exam at IU. In fact he was going in search of a good lawyer, with a stop at the scene of his alleged crime. Myriam returned from the police station Wednesday night "completely depleted and traumatized," said Maureen. "We sat in the kitchen and talked with her. The next morning she left to meet with an attorney, and I think she had an appointment with a representative of the Civil Liberties Union."

Myriam was in a sort of double jeopardy, at risk not only of conviction on drug charges but also, as a non-citizen, deportation. She was back from the lawyers when Chuck came to the door around noon. He appeared ill and headed straight to the bathroom. After 10 minutes Myriam went to the door and asked if he was okay. Getting no answer, she opened the door and smoke billowed out.

Chuck was burning papers, apparently letters, and color photos in the bathtub and trying to flush the ashes in the toilet. The photos were of a young, dark-skinned boy Myriam thought resembled Tony. She asked Chuck to clean up the mess and take it outside. He seemed hesitant to talk inside the house, as if it was bugged. When they were outside he turned to Myriam and said, "Tony betrayed me."

In early afternoon Chuck went to the downtown office of Dick Wilder, a criminal defense attorney with a nose for hard cases and brouhahas who published a weekly paper, the *Star Courier*, that local attorneys opened with trembling fingers. Chuck spent three hours with Wilder. He thought Chuck was abnormally calm given the gravity of the charges.

During the meeting, Wilder's secretary took a call for Chuck. She stepped into the room and handed Chuck the message. It was from Myriam. Chuck read it aloud to Wilder: 'Bruno and I want to talk to you when you're through with your attorney.' Chuck asked Wilder what he made of the note. He wouldn't venture a guess about their motives. It's a free country, Wilder said, you can do what you want.

Chuck folded the note and put it in the pocket of his short-sleeve shirt. He left Wilder's office around 4:30. On the way back to Myriam's home he stopped to chat with Kent Harvey at one of the houses he was painting that summer. Harvey recounted their brief exchange in a letter to a friend:

"He came over to tell me about his arrest, and subsequent developments, and expressed optimism that he would be able to leave town in August. He also said he was innocent of the charge, and I'm quite sure, from talking to other people involved, that in the incident which caused his arrest, he was in fact not guilty of possessing."

By that time Bloomington's two dailies had hit the streets with short front-page stories. Under the headline "Charged with Pot," the *Courier-*

Tribune story noted that "Mrs. Champigny is the wife of Professor Robert Champigny, research professor of French at Indiana University. Walls is listed as a graduate student in the school of eduction at Indiana University." Both papers reported that a 15-year- old boy in the house was taken into custody and was expected to be turned over to juvenile authorities.

It was late afternoon and Chuck had promises to keep. He would be halfway home to Bedford by now for the oft-postponed photo shoot with Sally, if not for the cryptic note from Myriam. "I'm sure he wanted to know, 'Why do they want me coming by, what is it they could possibly say?'" Sally said. "Is it something that could help me?'"

He arrived at the Champigny home to find only Bruno and Maureen. They said Myriam was visiting a neighbor, Alfred Lindesmith, an IU sociology professor. He was a leading scholar on the nature of addiction who had just published a book, *The Addict and the Law*. She had asked them to stick around and keep Chuck company.

"He told us he was busy writing, and he was," Bruno said. "He showed us a page of his script—tiny, minuscule little things. It was a full page, not a note. He said he was going to continue writing in his room."

"He looked terrible," Maureen said. "We tried to engage him in conversation. I was fixing pasta for Bruno and me and offered him some. He said he had a phone call to make and walked down the hall to the bedroom at the back of the house where there was a phone. He came back to the kitchen, took something to drink, and I offered again to have him join us at the table.

"He said, 'No, I have some more phone calls to make.' Then he went to the bedroom on the other side of the hall, in the front of the house, and closed the door. I thought it odd that he went there because there was no phone in that room."

A few minutes later, a loud *pop* resounded through the house.

"We thought it was a firecracker being thrown at the house," Maureen said. "Then we both knew."

They ran down the hall and banged on the door repeatedly, frantic. Finally, Bruno broke down the door.

"We found him there, lying on the bed," Maureen said. "He had taken his shirt off and fired a bullet through his heart. He had clearly made sure the gunshot was going to end his life. Bruno found no pulse. Charles died immediately."

Police received a call at 5:12 p.m. from Maureen reporting that a man had been shot. It was less than a hour since Chuck had left Wilder's office and spoken optimistically about the future with Harvey.

Police told the press that a Smith & Wesson .38-caliber Airweight with a 2-inch barrel was found on the floor between the bed and the wall. It was the same gun that Chief of Detectives Russell Parks said he found just the night before at the bust. It was in a drawer, wrapped in brown paper "in the box it came in." It was registered to Robert but no permit to carry had been issued. Apparently, Parks inspected the gun and put it back in the drawer where Chuck found it.

Parks said Walls "apparently was lying on a bed when the bullet entered his heart," the *Herald-Telephone* reported. "The bullet lodged in the mattress of the bed after it passed through the victim's chest, pierced his heart, and exited at a point in the middle of the back. 'He was sitting on the same bed listening to records when we arrested him Wednesday night,' Parks said."

The record he was listening to with Tony was the Beatles' masterwork. One song still haunts Tony. "I don't know the name of it, but it's *Sgt. Pepper's*, and there's one place where the sound drops—always reminds me of Chuck killin' himself. Or being shot. 'A Day in the Life'... yeah, that's it."

Police found Chuck's neatly pressed shirt hanging on a bedpost, but did not report retrieving a folded note from the pocket. Given Chuck's proclivity for revealing intimate emotions in prose, the absence of a parting note surprised everyone. "There was no suicide note in either bedroom," Maureen said. "Bruno looked." Also conspicuously absent from the police report was the writing Chuck was so engrossed in when he arrived at the house—an image Bruno recalls vividly to this day, "...It was a full page, not a note."

When Myriam returned from Professor Lindesmith's home and learned Chuck was dead, she collapsed. Robert was still en route home from California. Around 8:30 p.m. Myriam was admitted to Bloomington Hospital. The news hadn't reached Bedford. Sally was still waiting for her close-up with Chuck in his black turtleneck.

That night, August 8, was the final night of the Republican National Convention in Miami Beach. The Nixon-Agnew ticket was being anointed in prime time. Sally was the only one in the Walls living room not celebrating.

"I was a rebellious Democrat even at 14, trying to watch with my mother, her mother and my sister (Mary Beth)," Sally said. "I was waiting for Chuck to get home so I could vent my disgust because we were still devastated by the loss of Bobby Kennedy.

"We were sitting in this bedroom/TV room that faced the front door. Just as Nixon and Agnew were raising their arms in solidarity I saw headlights come through the curtain. I pulled the curtain back and saw a state police car. And I knew it was bad. Mom said, 'Who is it?' I told her and she jumped up and ran out. Moments later I heard a gut-wrenching cry, almost a scream."

At the door were two neighbors, a doctor's wife and an Indiana State policeman, both parishioners of Rev. Walls, who was in Terre Haute that night. He had gone to visit his mother before the family left Monday to drive Chuck to California.

"They said there's been a terrible accident and Mom thought they said, 'It's Jack' and she asked if he was all right. They had to stop her and say, 'No, it's not Jack. It's Chuck.' And she collapsed into her mother's arms."

The neighbors took Shirley Walls to Bloomington to identify Chuck's body. "It was the hardest thing she ever had to do," Sally said. On the way they told her Chuck's fatal wound was self-inflicted. "She didn't believe them." Afterward they drove to Terre Haute to pick up Rev. Walls and his mother.

At the home in Bedford, Sally was left to her own devices. Her other grandmother Wilma, Shirley's mom, "couldn't speak, she was just walking around." Sally still hadn't cried. "I couldn't cry. Crying made it real, and it couldn't be real. Not my brother, my mentor, my best friend.

"Some neighbors from the church came down and got Mary Beth so they can take her up to their house and console her. I got someone from the church who came in and said, 'Sally, let's go in the kitchen and do all these dinner dishes. It's going to be so nice for your mom when she comes home and you've done the dishes.' That's it, that's what I got.

"I'm standing in the kitchen, and there's a light where it comes down the hill, and these well-meaning neighbors are taking my sister—they've got their arms around her—they're taking her up to their house. And I'm hearing this woman drone on and on, and I'm in the kitchen washing dishes. That's what I got.

"My father was sedated after coming home. He was not strong, not capable of being there for my mother. They came close to divorcing that winter. My mother had no one who could help her, so I grew up quickly and stepped into that role. My childhood was over, and I never looked back."

Yesterday

*J*n 1968, before the internet and cable TV and 24-hour news, people in places like Bloomington got the news from afternoon newspapers that paperboys rolled up with rubber bands and tossed on front porches. Most readers didn't look at the paper until after work and dinner.

Thursday evening when they saw the brief page-one story about a high school teacher arrested Wednesday for possession of drugs, they had no idea they were reading about a dead man. Chuck was declared dead Thursday afternoon before most of them sat down to dinner. Outside of the police, Myriam, and the Civiticos, almost no one was aware of the fatal denouement that day.

George Wilder, 13, had an early private channel to the news Thursday through his father, Dick Wilder, Chuck's attorney.

"I had just mowed the lawn at our house," George said. "It was sort of late afternoon, cooling off, going into the evening. Dad was late. When he got home he was upset by what had happened. He wasn't crying but he was visibly upset, shaken. I never saw my dad that way. I think he wished this young man had held on because he felt he could have gotten him a good result in the case."

Not even Tony knew until the day after. The last time he saw Chuck they both were being led away from the Champigny home in handcuffs. "It was so strange how I found out how he killed himself." Friday morning, in a surreal transition from the momentous to the mundane, Tony went to drivers ed class. With him in the car were friends who knew some of what had happened. The instructor was the BHS football coach, Fred Huff.

"We were driving around town and it came on the radio about Chuck killing himself. One of my friends looked at me like, 'Oh shit!' I was sick, just sick."

When the car returned to school at the end of the class, Tony was distraught. He sought out band director Traub, who also had training as a counselor. "He came rushing into my office and wanted to talk in the music library for privacy," Traub said. "He was in tears."

Traub felt that Tony was mistreated by police, "The law did some arm twisting that shouldn't have been done," and he had been exploited by Myriam. "Tony was a boy toy. He was put in a position beyond a 15-year-old's ability to make decisions. He was being *used* by this woman."

One of Chuck's closest friends, a BHS girl he used to slip playful love notes, heard the news from her grandmother. "I was at home. She was driving our car that morning and heard the story on the radio. She came right over to tell me. She meant to be a comforting presence, but it was not good. 'I have something to tell you: Chuck killed himself.' I screamed. It was the end of the world."

Anne Schmitz, daughter of a philosophy professor, had a strong affinity for her teacher as someone like herself who was on a quest for meaning. She was crushed when she heard the news while visiting a friend.

"I immediately left and biked home. I was really heartbroken. I remember riding and thinking, 'Holy crap.' It was just so shocking to me because we related so closely to his kind of adolescent spirit. I thought, 'Hell, if he can do it, I can do it, too.' It was a real crack."

Word of the killing rippled through the community on radio and in the Friday afternoon newspapers ("Marijuana Case Suspect Is Dead"). Some students of Chuck learned the news from parents who worked at IU where the grapevine lit up with reports of a tragedy involving a professor and his wife.

Pam Lawrence, a future teacher, said Chuck gave her "the crystal clear knowledge as a 16-year-old of what I was intended to do with my life." That black Friday, "My mother called me from the IU School of Education where she worked to let me know of his death before I heard it elsewhere. She knew what he meant to me."

Lawrence phoned Heidi Remak in Vermont where she was attending Ecole Champlain, a summer French camp. They both had Chuck for sophomore English and were extras in the classroom production starring Tony as Julius Caesar. "I was called to the office for a phone call," Remak said. "I remember the office was in a white house, and I remember walking out of the office after speaking with Pam. She told me Mr. Walls committed suicide after saying, 'Tony betrayed me.'"

Cathy Hoff had traveled to Oxford with Chuck and returned transformed, on a path to becoming an English professor. Chuck would sometimes visit her home to talk with her dad about music and books and ideas.

"My parents told me about his death. They were journalists and very clued in to the community. My father probably knew before it got in the newspaper because he was editor of the IU News Bureau. It was a total shock to me, but that says more about me at that age. I was very naive."

Except for Tony, no student had a more fraught relationship with Chuck than did Jana Kellar. It was her parents' discovery of her diary with entries about Chuck that triggered a rush of falling dominos climaxing in the events of August 8. Kellar was in West Lafayette where her father, an IU archaeologist, was running a field school at the site of an early French trading post.

"I was in the field doing archaeology. I'd done it since I was 14," she said. "Somebody called my parents and they told me. I was speechless. I know my mother got upset because I didn't cry. There are some things that are so overwhelming that there is no emotional reaction." (Kellar could not bring herself to attend Chuck's funeral.)

Ann and Jim McGarrell were in Vermont after a trip to France. Ann was in the dark the day she picked up the phone to call Myriam.

"I had sent her something from France, a children's book, and wanted to see if she had received it. She sounded both distraught and distracted. Clearly something was wrong. I became very worried. She was not weeping but she was not herself. Not in her cadence of speech. She didn't want me to speak French, afraid it would be overheard and mistranslated. It became clear she thought the phone was being monitored. I said, 'Did someone die or is someone dead?' She said, 'Yes, it was someone who was not important to me in life but now he is."

The network of Chuck's friends, acquaintances and acolytes was far-flung that summer. Alan Thomas, who had introduced Chuck to Myriam, was in the middle of the Atlantic on a cruise ship headed for Athens when he got the news.

"I was sitting in the bar, of course, and someone came up and said, 'Alan!' It was two friends. They had just gotten married and they said, 'You know Chuck killed himself.' At first I thought it was another Chuck, and she said, 'No, no—the Chuck who was a school teacher.' I immediately sent Myriam a telegram and told her I would be glad to return if there was a problem. I never heard from her."

Julia Wrubel, headed for Swarthmore in the fall, was spending time in New Mexico where her father, an astrophysicist, was working at the Los Alamos Scientific Laboratory.

"Catherine (Hoff) called me. I can picture myself standing in the room where the phone was and getting the call. I want to say it was evening. I thought he had killed himself in a jail cell. It was such a terrible time. Everybody was dying."

In a diary entry for Friday, August 9, 1968, she wrote: "I just can't believe it. It just isn't right that being arrested for illegal possession of marijuana could cause him to take his own life. There must have been some other reasons. I keep thinking that she was talking about someone else, not Chuck."

Gail Herr had spent all day Wednesday, August 7, waiting for a promised call from Chuck as she reflected on their idyllic days at Oxford the summer before. In her diary she wrote, "Margaret and I are having a wine and cheese party for our special friends here in Vermont now that this wonderful summer is nearly over and I am waiting for Chuck's phone call which never comes."

Several days later, Gail's fiancé drove her home to the suburbs of Washington D.C.

"We walked into the apartment and it couldn't have been more than a minute or two that the phone started ringing. I left him sitting in the living room and went into my bedroom and picked up the phone. Kathy Bogner was saying, 'Gail, where have you been? I've been trying to reach you for days and there's been no answer.' I asked what was going on, what happened? I don't remember her exact words, but it was that Chuck is dead. He has been shot. My fiancé knew that Chuck and I were great friends. We both agreed I needed to go out to Indiana. My fiancé told me, '*I* wouldn't be going to a funeral. I would be out looking for that son of a bitch [who shot him].'"

The hardest blow reached the farthest back. In Chuck's awkward years at Seymour High as a gay nerd trying to find his way among farmers and jocks, his best friend was Dena Klein. "Chuck was like another brother," she said. They crossed paths at Evansville College but when Chuck transferred to IU they lost touch. After traveling many rough roads, Klein returned to Seymour in 1968.

"I was going through horrible things in my life. An abusive man who burned me with water. I came home in the middle of June with my 2-year-old daughter. Then I heard about Chuck."

The story ran in the August 10 edition of the *Seymour Daily Tribune* under the headline, "Former Resident Takes Life At Bloomington."

"It hit me so hard," Klein said. "Chuck was a special person in my life. It was that brotherly closeness. He had so much to offer. I just knew he would aways be all right. I was devastated."

Two days after Chuck died, a letter arrived at Wrubel's home in Los Alamos, NM. It was from Chuck, dated August 6, the day before the bust. Written in his diminutive cursive from his parents' home in Bedford, it was classic Chuck:

"Dear Julia,

"Meant to mail this yesterday so you could surely reply before I leave, which will be Monday. If you mail a missive airmail Sat. morning, I may get it.

"Our second and last Soul Picnic will be Sunday afternoon. My final is Friday. Then last packing—what a hassle—then see *2001* Saturday.

"Janis Joplin [of Big Brother and the Holding Co.] was on Dick Cavett Monday a week ago and mentioned forthcoming LP *Cheap Thrills*, title of which was reduced from 'Dope, Sex and Cheap Thrills' by Columbia Records. 'I mean, who could be against *that?!*' she exclaimed. [principal] John T. [Jones], I replied...

"Other promising LPs scheduled for immediate release include Stones' *Beggar's Banquet*, new Jimi Hendrix Experience [*Electric Ladyland*], Peter, Paul and Mary *Late Again* and *Anthem of the Sun* by the Grateful Dead.

"Did you read of James Brown's stirring endorsement of HH [Hubert Humphrey] in Watts? He then started singing soulfully and Hubie shouted into the mike, 'So good!' and then proceeded in a soul chant (oooo-ahhh) which he put backwards (ahhh-oooo).

"Your cartoon was a classic gas. Enclosed is your freakiest pinup of the week. [A Ronald Reagan campaign poster.] Life in NM sounds not utopian, but I know you will cope. Kent, having sent you a very groovy tape, is planning to try to see you at O'Hare.

"Sloth and envy? Lorraine Fish and Janis Joplin? Abigail Williams and Yossarian? Yossarian and Hungry Joe? Hungry Joe and Country Joe? Randle P. McMurphy and Big Nurse? Mama Cass and Pigpen?

"Hope your column ['BHS Panther Looks Back'] materializes. With Gosser in charge it might not be blessed, so feel free to tell Peggy Pruett— a conventional middle-class yet progressively inclined and favorable to me editor in chief—that the idea has my full blessing.

"Hope you've caught the biggest entertainment of the whole Repub. Conv. - nightly Wm. Buckley-Gore Vidal insult fests. Really a groove.

"Keep in touch. Write me and mail me a letter Friday nite. You may NOT call me Charles! It must be...Chuck"

Photos Shown In Champigny Trial

FRIDAY, JUNE 13, 1969

(Continued from Page 1)

general reputation of being a homosexual.

Judge Donald A. Rogers granted a court recess early Thursday afternoon at the request of the prosecutor, who declared the State had come upon newly discovered evidence in the middle of his cross-examination of defendant Myriam Champigny.

Mrs. Champigny was on the stand almost the entire day Thursday, beginning her defense testimony during the morning session. Under cross examination she testified that Charles Walls appeared at her home around 11 a.m. Aug. 8, the day after their arrest, and went into her bathroom, where he remained for up to 15 minutes.

Thinking he was ill, she said, she entered the bathroom and found it full of smoke. Walls, she testified,

was burning what appeared to be personal papers in her bathtub, and on top was a photograph of a dark boy whom, she said, she thought could be Tony Solomito. Walls explained that he had tried to flush the papers down the toilet, but they would not go down.

Mrs. Champigny further testified that she asked Walls to take the burning papers outside, which he did. When he returned, she said, he seemed afraid to talk in the house, indicating he thought it might be bugged. She said she and Walls went outside, where he told her, "I'm sorry I got you into this — you're the victim of circumstances."

Area Deaths

Charles Walls

Charles Ancil Walls III, 23, of 1945 N. College, who died Thursday afternoon at 5 p.m. in the home of Mr. and Mrs. Robert Champigny, 1040 Maxwell Lane, of an apparently self-inflicted gunshot wound.

Born in Evansville on Sept. 6, 1944, he was the son of Charles and Shirley Burton Walls. He was a former English teacher at Bloomington High School.

Surviving in addition to his parents, are two sisters, Mary Beth and Sally, both at home; his paternal grandmother, Mrs. Maysell Beal of Terre Haute; maternal grandmother, Mrs. Wilma Stitt of Greencastle; one aunt and several cousins.

He was a member of the First Methodist Church of Bloomington, where the funeral will be held at 10:30 a.m. Monday. Dr. Richard Hamilton and Dr. Robert Gingery will officiate, and burial will be in Center Ridge Cemetery at Sullivan. Friends may call at the Ferguson-Lee Funeral Home in Bedford after 6 p.m. Saturday, and at the church for one hour preceding the service Monday.

Chuck
1944—1968

Daily Herald-Telephone [Champigny trial news clip, June 13, 1969] and Chuck Walls Obituary August 9, 1968 [Photo *Gothic* 1968]

Charles Ancil Walls III, 23, of 1945 N. College, who died Thursday afternoon at 5 p.m. in the home of Mr. and Mrs. Robert Champigny, 1040 Maxwell Lane, of an apparently self-inflicted gunshot wound.

Born in Evansville on Sept. 6, 1944, he was the son of Charles and Shirley Burton Walls. He was a former English teacher at Bloomington High School.

Surviving in addition to his parents, who now reside in Bedford, are two sisters, Mary Beth and Sally, both at home; his paternal grandmother, Mrs. Maysell Beal of Terre Haute; maternal grandmother, Mrs. Wilma Stitt of Greencastle; one aunt and several cousins.

He was a member of the First Methodist Church of Bloomington, where the funeral will be held at 10:30 a.m. Monday. Dr. Richard Hamilton and Dr. Robert Gingery will officiate, and burial will be in Center Ridge Cemetery at Sullivan. Friends may call at the Ferguson-Lee Funeral Home in Bedford after 6 p.m. Saturday, and at the church for one hour preceding the service Monday.

The man I might have been

huck's funeral was scheduled for Monday, August 12, the day he had planned to leave for California. The final arrangements reflected his unrooted life as the son of a minister moved from town to town by the Methodist powers that be.

Visitation and viewing of the body was at Ferguson-Lee Funeral Home in Bedford, his parents' home of just three months. The open-casket funeral service was at First Methodist Church in Bloomington where he was a member. Burial would be in Sullivan where his father had been pastor but Chuck had never lived.

It was hard to tell that the mourners gathered in the sanctuary of the majestic church were there for the funeral of a 23-year-old.

"There were a lot of people there, but people who knew my parents from Seymour and Sullivan," Sally said. "I was looking for people I knew that Chuck knew. I didn't see them. I don't know why they were afraid to come."

The Civiticos came, "thinking it was showing him respect," Maureen said, but there were hard feelings. Chuck's family "snubbed us and were said to have told people we had something to do with 'dope dealers' and possibly his death. The near nervous breakdown I had after all of this— especially after finding Charles' body—changed my life indelibly. I couldn't eat or sleep for weeks and it was many months before I could sleep without having terrible nightmares."

Sally was put off by Bruno's attire. "I remember looking down and thinking, 'What kind of guy wears a suit and open sandals to a funeral?'"

There were a few of Chuck's people: Gail Herr, Bob Deppe, Peggy Pruett, Wally Brazy. But in the church they were Waldos in a sea of faces that were mostly strangers to Chuck. Many more were not there, some possibly because they were too far away, though Deppe and Herr traveled from the east coast. A greater deterrent than distance was fear.

"I wasn't allowed to go," said one girl, a confidante of Chuck's forced to keep her distance (even now by anonymity.) "My parents—oh my God. They wanted me to have nothing to do with it because he was into drugs. They didn't want their perfect little daughter or their reputation besmirched or involved in any way."

The tale of drugs, suicide, a school teacher, an underage student and French professor's wife was sensational for Bloomington. It ran on the front page next to a story headlined "Champion Steer Brings $804.75."

"My parents were either urging or requiring me to stay away from everything having to do with him [Chuck] by then, or I figured out the advisability of that on my own," said Veronica Sebeok. "They were concerned, conceivably rightly, there could be a witch hunt and I would be suspected by association. At that point their priority was getting me off to college without incident."

Brazy assumed the witch hunt had already begun and came anyway. "I couldn't miss the funeral. I was up in South Bend and I had to come back down. Of course, I think we were all investigated by the F.B.I. if we signed the guest list at the funeral. We were sure of that."

That week both Bloomington dailies published a 600-word appreciation of Chuck which began: "A 'real teacher' is the way one of his former students at Bloomington High School referred to Mr. Walls, who gave of himself to the profession of teaching," and concluded: "For those who knew Chuck Walls best, his death is a great loss...for he was not only beloved by his family but by his students who because of his understanding and concern looked upon him as a friend as well as a teacher." It was signed, "A Friend"

The *Herald-Telephone* ran a letter which was a long primal-scream excoriating marijuana laws. "How many more victims are we to have? How many more suicides, arrests, ruined careers are required before the American public becomes aware of the fact it is being deceived by a 'drug fiend' myth directed at marijuana users by manufacturers of liquor and cigarettes?" That writer, too, was anonymous "for I fear, with the justified paranoia typical of today's youth, that I might be arrested by federal agents if my identity were known."

A long, contentious Editor's Note, rare in the letter-to-the-editor section, replied in part: "Knowing the law and the penalties, you have only yourself to blame if you are 'subjected' to paranoia and fear. If the laws against marijuana are wrong, certainly they should be changed. But, in the meantime, it just doesn't make sense to break the law."

Paranoia and fear were not confined to contemporaries of Chuck. Don Beaver, his history teacher at Seymour High and a colleague at BHS, was a pallbearer at the funeral, but not without trepidation. "I was concerned about my job."

Gail flew in from her home near Washington D.C. and met up with Kathy Bogner. They'd become good friends at Oxford in the summer of '67. Saturday night in advance of the service they traveled to Bedford for visitation at the funeral home. Among those who signed the guest book was Ed Whitcomb, Indiana secretary of state and later governor, a Methodist from a small town two counties away. Rev. Walls had friends in high places.

The family had chosen a $1,000 package, including the casket. Chuck was laid out in a Batesville 20-Gauge Steel Monogard model. "Whoever prepared him did a very good job," Gail said. "He looked exactly as he did when he was alive. I think Chuck is the last dead person I ever viewed."

Gail drove on the return trip to Bloomington, 25 miles through farm land and limestone outcroppings on highway 37.

"It was dusk when we left to head back and there was little to no traffic on the road other than us," Bogner said. "After a while I noticed there was a car following us at the same distance for what seemed like a long way. I told Gail, 'I think we're being followed.' It was a state trooper. He stopped us and asked a few questions and let us go. I remember him shining his flashlight at us. It was frightening. We drove the rest of the way back to Bloomington without saying a word."

Bogner decided not to attend the funeral. "It seemed anyone associated with Chuck was being watched." Tony also stayed away. "I didn't think it would be appropriate." And paranoia had begun to burrow into his psyche, planted there by police.

A detective told him that "details in the paper weren't accurate but they didn't want the information out," Tony said. "He told me to be paranoid because they didn't really think Chuck had killed himself. He also said that in front of my parents."

Gail didn't buy the official finding of suicide, based purely on her instinct. "I felt so sure Chuck did not commit suicide because we were scheduled to talk the same day. The way Chuck felt about me, if he was going to shoot himself he would have waited until we talked."

Her suspicions aroused, Gail visited Bloomington police headquarters to ask questions—only to become the object of suspicion.

"Keep in mind, this was 1968 and I was a very attractive woman. I had spent time on the beach and I was tanned and I had waist-length red hair. I walked into the police station and asked about Chuck. Oh yeah, they got very interested, and I was taken into an officer's office.

"When I told who I was, that I was a good friend of Chuck Walls, they said we need to know why you were at the funeral, all the way from D.C. I told them he was a good friend. They said, are you trying to tell us that you came all the way out here from D.C. for just a friend? To a '60s person that is a shocking thing to say because a friend is everything."

Deppe was at his family's summer home in Cape Cod when he learned Chuck had died. "I never had taken a class from him. I had partied with him one single time. I had talked to him between classes. I did not know him that well."

Yet, there never was a question he would come to Bloomington for the funeral. It was a parting gesture of gratitude and solidarity.

"There were the Jill Carraways and other teachers who were kind and maybe a little saner ultimately than Chuck," Deppe said, "but he was the one who was most visibly standing up for us when the school was seeming to be a repressive place."

It may also have been a sense of moral accountability which impelled Deppe to come a thousand miles. A what-if bedeviled him: What if he had not enlisted classmates to lie and free Chuck from suspension in the fall of 1967? Would he still be alive?

"I felt I had done a good thing even though technically it was wrong—until I heard he committed suicide. Then I began second-guessing. If I hadn't lied and helped him get back, would he have learned his lesson and somehow changed things? We don't know. Since the suicide I've never been able to feel I did a good thing."

"I remember being surprised it was such a conventional funeral," Gail said.

Officiated by two veteran ministers, it was a stately, traditional service that probably suited the taste of the Rev. and Mrs. Walls' Methodist cohort that filled most of the pews.

The organist, Charles Webb from the Indiana University School of Music, played a a series of hymns: "Come, Sweet Death" (Bach), "A Mighty Fortress is our God" (Martin Luther), "Our Help in Ages Past," "Oh, For a Faith That Will Not Shrink," and the Doxology. Webb, a frequent participant in local funerals, received his standard $15 fee.

Had Chuck been able to plan his own service he no doubt would have included some non-devotional music from the 20th century meaningful to him. Maybe "Bridge Over Troubled Waters" or "Let it Be," and at least one speaker from his own generation. It felt like the funeral for an 80-year-old church deacon.

For some who stayed away, the hurt was too deep to expose in a public place. "It was private for me," said Anne Schmitz, who had conflicted feelings about Chuck. "Losing him scared me so much. I don't know that I wanted to show anything to anybody about him."

Beyond the grief and paranoia was a sense of betrayal among people who had invested so much hope and belief in Chuck as an exemplar of '60s iconoclasm. He was their surrogate rebel with a cause. As Tony had betrayed him to the police, so had Chuck betrayed them, squandering his gifts and their trust through inexplicable recklessness.

Blair, the plain-talking big sister Chuck never had, saw this day coming, dreaded it, did all in her power to stop it. For two years she begged Chuck to cut his hair, bite his tongue, curtail his risky behavior with students—do whatever necessary to placate his antagonists in the front office.

"When I heard he was busted I thought, 'Oh my God, he crossed the line.' I was so angry at him. I was angry because he really had a choice, but he would not make the compromises. He could have been a compelling force for change. Those kids deserved him. I was so angry. Honestly, I didn't really have a lot of compassion for him at that point."

Al King said: "I was looking for a way to understand what it is to be a successful adult gay man, and when he died I was, like, wow. At that time, if you saw a gay person, a caricature, in a movie or anything, they always died. And so when he died it was a dark place for me. You know, gay men don't live, we die. How am I ever going to be successful?"

Schmitz's father, Kenneth, had written, and signed, a letter to the *Herald-Telephone* in praise of Chuck after his death: "I only met Mr. Walls once, and can say nothing about his alleged activities. Nevertheless, I came to know him indirectly through his stimulating influence upon my daughter's study of English. I saw in his guidance the heart and mind of a sensitive and creative young teacher. For those who sensed his appreciation of literature, his obituary should read: He taught well."

But losing the teacher who revealed to her the magic of literature was not the reason Chuck's death left Schmitz in a kind of existential rage and mourning.

"We all speculated that he was going to prison and that's why he killed himself. Of course we knew the real reason. We just didn't want to say it. He was weak. All of his conviction wasn't real. That's scary when you're in the middle of social change like we were. I went from thinking at five that I would marry someone and have kids and be a wife for the rest of my life, to knowing at 16 I had to go out there, get a job, take care of myself. I can't be dependent on a man. My whole future identity had changed. This guy comes along and says, 'This is good, embrace the social change, this is the way you think, you're not just a young lady, you're a person.' And then to see him just crumble at the first big wave was devastating, even though we knew he was vulnerable and weak and didn't have solid self-identity. He was still our symbol."

For Deppe he was the stuff of poetry, a palette of clashing colors. "I tried four or five times. The early poems were very sort of hagiography: 'St. Chuck destroyed by the system.' Then there came a point when I was really angry at him. It wasn't without admiration or love, but feeling he had let us down, that he had a chance, that we had stuck our necks out for him and he had gone back into the same place by going right back into drugs and allowing himself to be caught with students."

Nora Leill, a student who barely survived her trip down the psychedelic rabbit hole and observed Chuck's from a distance, said, "I stopped all drugs when I was 20. I think I realized that you're born with a certain amount of grace, like in a bank account, and you can run that dry pretty quickly, and after that's gone there's no more grace. You just have to stop."

Chuck could not—or would not. At the end, he left his closest friends angry and bereft. At the church, in a bizarre pas de deux in the receiving line, his family and Gail were left to enact the charade he had fostered that he was straight and that Gail was a woman he could marry.

"I had no idea how close Chuck was with his family. I didn't think they'd know very much about me," she said. "So I went down the line to tell them who I was, and as soon as Chuck's father heard me say my name he said, 'Gail. Are you Gail? Shirley! Gail is here!'

"The whole family knew about me. They were absolutely ripped open with their grief. They said, 'Can you come visit us in our home tonight? Maybe you can help us deal with this.' They showed me a picture of me and Chuck together and said it was his favorite picture. His grandmother looked at me and said, 'You know, all of us love you because he loved you so much.' I was just stunned."

Deppe left the funeral thinking, "He looked waxed, totally unlike himself. I was horrified," and went to the home of a classmate from the Class of '68, forbidden by her parents to attend the funeral.

"She was really upset, taking it very hard," Deppe said. "There were six or seven of us there. She had a ouija board and wanted to contact Chuck. I don't remember what it said but it was enough that it made me very uncomfortable. There was some communication. It was spooky."

No one there accompanied Chuck on his final earthly journey to Center Ridge Cemetery in Sullivan to be laid to rest. The pallbearers were six teachers: Don Beaver, Bill Sturbaum, Dale Scott, Bill Gosser, Joel Marsh, Gus Burchfield. They were the peer group of male colleagues Chuck never had or really wanted.

Maybe the students, his true peers, stayed away for fear of contracting his stigma, or police scrutiny. Perhaps it was the dread of their own mortality—that in witnessing Chuck's burial they would be experiencing the death of their own innocence.

The inscription on Chuck's headstone, a polished rectangle of speckled granite, reads "Beloved Son & Brother." It's a dispiritingly generic message of the sort he assiduously eschewed when signing yearbooks. Chuck always reached for higher meaning, for the intensely personal, for transcendence.

Only weeks earlier, he had prefaced his yearbook inscriptions to Remak and Pruett with Ernest Dowson's poem "They Are Not Long" (...*the weeping and the laughter...the days of wine and roses...*) He mistakenly labeled it as "Across the Fields of Yesterday," which is the first line of "Sometimes" by Thomas S. Jones, Jr.

Looking back, the erroneous citation seems prophetic, as if Chuck had glimpsed the rough beast slouching his way. And in his haunted prescience he had cited a poem worthy of his looming headstone, expressing the full beauty, sadness and transcendent truth of his life:

Across the fields of yesterday
He sometimes comes to me,
A little lad just back from play —
The lad I used to be.

And yet he smiles so wistfully
Once he has crept within,
I wonder if he hopes to see
The man I might have been.

EPILOGUE

*F*orty-seven years after Chuck died there, we knocked on the door at 1040 E. Maxwell Lane. Candy had contacted the residents a week before to say we were authors and asked if it would be okay to drop by. She told them that a drug bust had happened there in the summer of '68 and we would like to get a sense of the space we were writing about.

From outside, shrouded by the summertime verdancy of bushes and nodding trees, the house bore little resemblance to the home Myriam and Robert purchased in the late '50s. In an undated photo they are standing in a bare front yard, behind them the Lustron steel exterior they would later cover with brick.

The house was now owned by a couple with a young daughter. They cheerfully showed us around the interior which, except for furnishings, was much like the descriptions from people we had interviewed. When we entered the daughter's front bedroom, I blurted out, "This is where Chuck committed suicide." Candy stared at me in disbelief and I quickly moved on.

Half a century later many people who knew and loved Chuck still do not accept the coroner's finding that he killed himself in that room. A coterie of Myriam's friends continue to believe she was framed, that the marijuana police found in her home was planted there by Chuck or Tony or the police. Alternative scenarios abound on all sides.

Chuck was killed because he knew too much about the drug trade in Bloomington. No, it was a copycat suicide, inspired by a French film in which an older gay man kills himself after his young lover betrays him.

"Yes, yes, we thought Chuck is gay. We all later decided it [suicide] had to do with the movie," said Shehira Davezac.

Authorities have been unable to provide coroner and police reports on Chuck's death, including fingerprints and gun residue tests. (Ninety-year-old retired Detective Simes told us in 2014 that he didn't recall the tests being done.) In 1973, the court approved destruction of all evidence gathered for Myriam's trial. The total evidentiary vacuum has enabled the flowering of questions and theories which can never be refuted with finality.

Chuck died from a bullet to the heart, not the head or mouth, the sure-fire choices of most suicides. Even Berry, who believes Chuck killed himself, said "it's unusual; I've never encountered it before."

Chuck was left-handed. Why was the gun, a .38 caliber Smith & Wesson, allegedly found on the floor on the right side of the bed? "I thought it was a little strange the way he shot himself, the way his left hand was situated next to his body," said Detective Simes.

If Chuck shot himself, it is likely the first time he ever fired a gun, except for the toy six-shooter he is wielding—left-handed—as a cowboy with hat, chaps and lasso in a childhood snapshot. "Guns terrified him," Tony said. "One of the detectives told me he didn't think Chuck killed himself and said it was murder."

Why did Chuck, an inveterate writer who Bruno Civitico said was scribbling away minutes before his death, not leave a suicide note? "If he were going to do that, he wouldn't have *not* written a note to my mom," Sally said. "He just wouldn't."

And where were the scribbled notes? They might have held clues to many questions. Chuck's family was told by police that no writing of his was found at the scene.

Chuck Walls, age 5 [Courtesy of Sally Walls]

Chuck's shirt supposedly was found neatly draped over a bedpost. "If you're going to commit suicide, are you concerned whether or not your shirt is wrinkled?" Sally said. "Chuck was particular about his clothes and always ironed his shirts. Whenever he took a nap, he would hang up his shirt so it wouldn't be wrinkled when putting it back on."

At the time, police told the press that Chuck was lying on a bed when the bullet passed through his heart, exited his back, and was lodged in the mattress. In our interview, Simes said he found a bullet hole in the wall next to the bed. He also recounted how much he liked that .38 S&W Special revolver. A few months later he retrieved it from the evidence safe, looked up the owner by serial number and offered to buy it.

His memory is that he went to the "university apartment of the young man who was with Walls when I came to the [death] scene" and paid him for it. Simes made a holster for his shiny new pistol and carried it on his hip in the line of duty for several years but "never had to use it." The strange detail of prior ownership evokes more questions than we can resolve. Simes long ago resold the gun at a gun show.

The day Chuck died, the Civiticos told police they found Chuck lying on the bed. In separate 2014 interviews with us, Maureen echoed the original account, but Bruno described a very different scene.

"I opened the door and he was slumped back in his [desk] chair. I grabbed him by the shoulders, I looked at his face. His eyes were closed. His arms were dangling. His shirt was open. I moved him forward and saw that he had a bullet hole, a tiny hole, in his chest. I don't remember seeing a gun, but it must have been there somewhere."

Sally and family were not alone in doubting Chuck took his own life. The wide circle of disbelief included many former students.

"He did not commit suicide. He was killed. There is no doubt in my mind that's what happened," said Linda Aynes whose uncle, Harold Aynes, a Bloomington police detective, was in the raiding party that busted Chuck. "My understanding is that he was killed because of his sexual preferences."

During Bogner's and Gail's return to Bloomington after the visitation in Bedford, "Our conversation in the car was almost entirely about the fact that Chuck couldn't have, wouldn't have, killed himself," Bogner said.

Chuck posthumously lent credence to the skepticism in a note written to himself in the summer of '68. It was read at Myriam's trial by his mother, who found it among his belongings. "If they want to get rid of me, they will have to assassinate me," it said, with no mention of who "they" might be.

Fifty years later, Berry sees the lingering smoke but still no fire.

"He [Chuck] had essentially been fired. He's never gonna get another teaching job unless he lies. He was an addict. He was probably, almost certainly a homosexual. His suicide made perfect sense. If Dick [Wilder] thought for one moment that Chuck Walls had been killed, he would have been in my office. He would have said, 'Hey, you better look at this.'

"What you've got is fairly common. A family trying to deny there was a suicide. It has a very bad odor and connotation in our society. No family likes to admit it. They would much prefer murder. They are not making it up. They want to believe it, and they'll die believing it. Their sincerity is not at issue. What is at issue are the facts. There is no motive for anyone to kill Chuck."

This is not to say Berry has a clear conscience. He recalls his days as a swashbuckling pot buster with remorse, much like Robert McNamara, defense secretary under President Johnson, who issued a sorrowful mea culpa in *Fog of War* for his hawkish management of the Vietnam War.

"There is no question I am directly responsible for Chuck Walls' death," Berry told us. "I was a zealot, and I'm embarrassed about it. I look back and think, 'You've been wrong about a lot of things in your life, pal, but that's about No. 1.' I handled this case all wrong. If I had it to do over, I would have slid this thing under the rug. I know how I could have done it."

Today, Berry supports legalization of marijuana. While prosecutor he grew weary of charging pot heads and nickel-dime dealers with felonies and worked to change state law so prosecutors had the option of charging them with misdemeanors. Berry's conversion came too late for Myriam, who already had endured her inquisition.

Myriam's non-jury trial in June 1969 before Monroe County Superior Court Judge Donald Rogers lasted four days. It packed the courtroom, made front-page headlines, and was pure torment for Myriam and the Walls family including Sally. (Robert was in France visiting his ill father and missed the trial.) "The whole tone of the prosecution was snide and hateful," said Ann McGarrell.

In his opening statement Berry told the judge, "The testimony will read like a 10-cent store novel, but it is fact."

The Rev. and Mrs. Walls and 14-year-old Sally learned of Chuck's sexual identity for the first time surrounded by strangers, through the disturbing testimony of a former parishioner. Berry displayed several Polaroids taken by Tony the day of the bust including one of Myriam in a negligee.

Defense questioning of Tony veered into seamy alleyways. "They asked me, do you masturbate, have you ever had sex with a girl, are you queer, who wrote *Lord of the Flies*? I couldn't have told you what the front of the Bible said. They wanted to make me into a pathological liar."

Myriam wept on the stand when questioned about Chuck's suicide. She denied ever smoking marijuana but said she had read about it to satisfy her "curious mind." She also admitted to fascination with flying saucers, ESP, LSD, and the moon. One day she arrived in court with a bandaged leg and told the judge she burned it on the exhaust pipe of a friend's motorcycle.

It was not a textbook display of jurisprudence. Ginny Peacock, a key state witness who allegedly supplied Myriam with weed, was not put on the

Myriam Champigny entering courtroom [*Daily Herald-Telephone* July 1, 1969] and
[news clip June 11, 1969]

stand because Berry saw her lunching one day with friends of Myriam.
McGarrell said Judge Rogers "kept falling asleep." A band of Myriam's IU
friends were in the peanut gallery each day. They were so certain she
would be exonerated they scheduled a victory party before the trial
began. None, apparently, was from the school of law.

"I had almost a slam-dunk case," Berry told us. "There were a few loose
ends but no prosecutor should have lost that case."

And that was without the material Tony withheld. "Tom Berry prepared
me and prepared me and prepared me," he said. "But there's things I
didn't tell him. There were other people that could have been hurt really
bad, that I didn't want involved in it. I wasn't gonna compromise them
for anything because they had never hurt me."

Tony Solomito [*Gothic* 1968] [*Daily Herald-Telephone* June 10, 1969]

Defense attorney John Cotner's strategy, a slender thread, was to discredit all of Tony's testimony by showing he lied about one thing—Chuck's sexual orientation. When Cotner asked if Chuck was a homosexual, Tony said no. He lied to spare the feelings of Chuck's parents in the courtroom.

"It's pretty hard seeing a preacher sitting in the courtroom. That's one of the reasons I never brought up the part about being molested by Chuck. I just didn't feel like it was right."

Cotner then called to the stand John Baker, an IU law student and future appellate court judge who told us in 2013 that Chuck "made a play for me" in Rev. Walls' church basement when they were teenagers in Aurora, Indiana. Baker testified that Chuck had a "general reputation in the community of being a homosexual."

Baker later encountered the Walls family in the hall outside the courtroom. "I think Rev. Walls never forgave me," Baker said. "He said, 'You didn't have to say what you knew. You could have said, 'I don't know.'" Sally's memory is that Baker "apologized to my parents. He told them, 'I shouldn't have said that.'"

Cotner won the point but lost the case. Judge Rogers found Myriam guilty of possessing and distributing marijuana, felonies carrying sentences of 2 to10 years in prison. He suspended the sentences, fined Myriam $300 and placed her on probation. But she remained in jeopardy. An international law made any non-citizen convicted of a narcotics charge subject to deportation.

Sally turned 15 the day of the verdict. "It was a good present for me," she said. Ironically, it was the only day Shirley didn't allow Sally to be in the courtroom. Meanwhile, the "victory" party for Myriam went ahead as scheduled.

After the trial, Cotner railed at the absurdity of the law. "An alien could commit murder or rob Brinks of one million dollars and not be deported, but it's mandatory if you are convicted on a marijuana charge."

He filed a motion for a new trial, by jury this time, but it never happened. Before the end of the year, Myriam gathered her 11 cats and decamped for Switzerland where her father was a national hero. She was granted citizenship and still resides there at age 96.

"I think what really did it was that somebody hung a dead cat on her fence," McGarrell said. "I think she saw quite clearly that she was going to be a figure of scandal in a small, conservative town. And the dead cat [not one of Myriam's] was the thing that pushed her to go because she was afraid her own cats would be attacked."

Veterinarian Harry Koeppen made a house call to vaccinate the cats and provide health certificates for the journey. McGarrell and another faculty wife, Constance Will, accompanied Myriam and her feline entourage to the Indianapolis airport. "One cat wouldn't come and I had to send her the next day," McGarrell said. "Myriam left behind some of the clothes she most dearly loved. A beautiful bra collection, lace over lace."

Robert kept his position at IU, spending half of each year in Blooming-ton and the rest in Switzerland with Myriam. In late 1969 he sold "La Maison des Chats" to Francis Valette, an assistant professor of French with young children. Valette, who spent most of 1968 and '69 in France, was unaware of the home's recent history as a crime scene. "We bought the house directly from Robert without the intervention of a realtor," Valette said. "This tragic event was never mentioned by Robert or by any-one else." Robert died of cancer in 1984 at age 61 in Switzerland.

When BHS students reported for the start of a new school year a month after Chuck's death, "it was like it never happened," said Bill Sturbaum. There was no acknowledgement in *The Optimist* that BHS had lost one of its most popular teachers over the summer—a grace note which could have been done without rehashing the lurid details.

Chuck was gone but not forgotten by administrators. They viewed him as an object lesson in the perils of free speech and as a threat to their belief—once offered to a disbelieving Deppe—that "You're not here in high school to learn to think."

Determined to muzzle *The Optimist,* which under Chuck had become a free-wheeling forum for the arts, politics, opinion and satire, they installed a compliant faculty advisor with orders to keep the paper on a short leash.

"They couldn't have hired anyone more different—very conservative," Pruett, editor that year, said of Chuck's mild-mannered successor, Sharon Wyman. "I really think she was told to rein in the newspaper because they didn't want editorials about Vietnam, they didn't want any of those things."

The Optimist returned to its age-old rut as the purveyor of benign high school ephemera. In early 1969, a group of students started an alternative paper, *The New American Mercury,* an unbridled full-frontal assault on the rules, regulations, sensibilities and politics of the BHS establishment. Mark Brickell, a former *Optimist* reporter and National Merit Scholar semifinalist, was the driving force.

"They were hammering down on what they saw as rebellion, really tightening up on *The Optimist,*" said Cathy May, a *Mercury* editor. "There was a sense that there was not a place for anything that deviated from the party line. A lot of things were happening in the country and here was a place for giving those things voice. We were throwing down a gauntlet."

Goss was so incensed by the first edition that he confiscated a copy from a member of his track team and ceremoniously ripped it to shreds in front of the students. The editors decided to mock him in the second issue by running a dotted line down the inside fold with the message "TEAR HERE, MR GOSS," suggesting he use it as confetti at the next track meet. Don Gest, an editor, said that right before going to press Brickell changed the dotted line to Morse Code that read: "Fuck Milne, Fuck Jones, Fuck Goss."

"I was a previous member of the student council and up for the National Honor Society," Gest said. "I took my name off that issue because I could see Mark getting into a little bit of trouble there. That's what saved me."

Brickell, Cathy May and three other editors—Eric Bennett, Charles Carper, Kevin Campbell—were suspended, effectively expelled since it was late spring and their credits for the semester were revoked. Bennett returned to BHS in the fall. The others finished high school elsewhere.

"What happens when you tighten down on adolescents?" May asked. "What do your kids say to you when you tighten down? That's what we did in a very immature way because we were immature."

In bound volumes of *The Optimist* at BHS, an edition from the fall of '66 has a photo of 15 new teachers, including "Mr. Charles Walls." Someone has taken a pen and scribbled little concentric circles across Chuck's face, as if to erase him from the picture. No other teacher is defaced.

An ugly coup de grâce by an administrator or old-guard teacher? An impulsive stroke of anger and heartbreak by one of Chuck's students? It seems anything but random. In any case, Chuck's legacy is too complex to be easily erased. It could be seen on Phil Schrodt's office door at the University of Pennsylvania where he taught political science. For years he posted quotes collected on 3x5 cards.

"Forty-five years later and that quote thing is still with me," Schrodt said. The quote he remembers from Chuck's blackboard was from John Donne's poem "No Man Is An Island." It ends, "And therefore never send to know for whom the bell tolls; it tolls for thee." At the time he thought the poem a "mundane" choice, Schrodt said, but now it seems "highly appropriate given how things worked out."

"If Chuck Walls has a lasting legacy, it's the lesson he taught a generation of kids about the impunity of youth and the cruelty of adult life," Paul

Gordon, Class of '68, told us at the outset of our research. "A teacher is an intensely political position and I was keenly aware that Mr. Walls was playing a very dangerous game, given the time and place. He was the first victim of a drug-war holocaust that thus far has claimed 40 million victims."

But his was much more than the legacy of a victim—of his own demons and of the forces fearful of what he represented. In his '68 *Gothic* inscription to Pam Lawrence, who became a teacher, Chuck quoted lines from Wordsworth's "Intimations of Immortality" including the poet's admonition to "...grieve not, rather find strength in what remains behind."

Lawrence speaks for many who passed through Chuck's life and classroom and celebrated what remains by enacting his ideas and ideals.

"Without a doubt the most powerful influence in my future career was the year I spent in the challenging, inspiring, thought-provoking classroom of Chuck Walls. I remember like it was yesterday. He created a hotbed of thinking, wondering, arguing, exploring, creating. He set us on fire to learn and valued each student's ideas, individuality, perspective and point of view.

"I was the lead teacher and ran one of the first alternative programs in Indiana. I think now of Mr. Walls asking us to have our 'approved texts' ready in case an administrator happened into the classroom. The connection between that and me teaching in a classroom where nothing had to be approved and we could make inspiring choices of material to fit our kids is probably not coincidental.

"I always laughed when my students chose *1984* or *Brave New World* for their novel units. We read both of those in Mr. Walls' class. I wrote quotes on the board, like he did, and my students who were encouraged to write journals often wrote about those quotes. I didn't ever think of giving Mr. Walls credit for that until many years later.

"Reflecting on Mr. Walls, I think of two lines from the great Pat Conroy: 'The great ones never leave me' and 'I steal from the great teachers.'

"I was a thief all those years, taking full credit for Mr. Walls' ideas, and he was there all along, I'm sure glad for the theft."

CODA

Since Virginia Elkin kicked Bob Deppe out of her creative writing class, he's written six books of poems. (He publishes under his given name, Theodore Deppe.) *Liminal Blue*, his latest, includes a lyric essay about Chuck Walls. Written in 2016, his essay revisits the Bloomington of the late '60s. In it, Bob finds that he misremembered some things, or didn't have the facts right to begin with. He writes: "The first thing I didn't know was that the bullet entered our high school English teacher's heart, not his brain—over the years, I've gotten that detail wrong in a series of poems." As the essay concludes, he wonders:

"By this point, have I let the anger go? Can I allow myself to see that young man, only 23, who, whatever his faults, did his best to teach his students in the midst of all that was most wrong and most joyful? I was living on Cape Clear Island off the coast of West Cork when I wrote my most recent poem about Chuck. Our house was high above the Atlantic, that great kingdom of flux that is lined with ruin. It seems somehow fitting to leave the last crucial detail wrong." He finishes his essay with that 2001 poem, reprinted with permission on the following page.

NIGHT TRAIN

I wake to the bent harmonica wail of a train, listen
to that childhood echo until I realize I'm on an island, eight miles
from the mainland. The unmistakable roll of countless wheels,

smooth glide of metal over metal, impossible
but passing relentlessly sleep's gate,
so I rise from bed, rush outside to understand.

Dense fog whips in, there's no way to see it, but the locomotive
churns by, just out of sight below the cliffs, until I know
it's the wind bringing close the sound of wheel-like waves.

And the whistle - surely the west wind's distorting
the lighthouse horn. Yes, which is not to say
the train's not out there, hundreds or thousands of cars long,

my wife's mother gazing from the window
into the North Atlantic fog, looking perhaps in my direction
though we can't quite see each other,

and Lynda Hull reciting lines into the smudged glass,
and David Dawson with three shades playing
Beethoven's quartet in A Minor, music for the deaf,

and James Merrill, looking up quizzically from his
    portable OED,
and—enough. It's cold out here. Back inside
to add coal to the fire. The house rocks in the wind,

hurrying somewhere. I think Chuck Walls
is on that train, still holding his gun in his lap, rubbing
the exit wound at his temple to see if it's started to heal.

—Theodore Deppe

ACKNOWLEDGMENTS

*W*e are grateful for Herald-Times editor Bob Zaltsberg's support for our effort to gain access to 1968 police files, and to former Bloomington mayor Mark Kruzan for making it happen. Jean Patteson, friend and former newspaper colleague, offered an astute critique of the manuscript and encouragement that helped us make it to the finish line of a four-year project. To Jeff and Darrell Ann Stone, thank you for loaning us your special "HeartStone Home" in Bloomington where we lived and conducted many interviews over three summers.

For this collective memoir we had contact with nearly 200 people in the course of our research. Many of those not quoted directly provided background woven into the narrative. Others confirmed or amplified information we already had, or directed us to new sources. Omitted from the list are three people who asked to be anonymous. Women are referred to by their names in high school. We thank each and every one of you. Your memories are the heart of this book.

Donna Adams, Sandy Alyea, Nancy Anderson, Beth Applegate, Laura Armstrong, Linda Aynes, Joe Baker, John Baker, Patty Baker, Nancy Barr, Doug Bauder, Don Beaver, Eric Bennett, Tom Berry, Virginia Berry, Nicole Bieganski, Allene Bilodeau, Dee Blair, Hedi Bouraoui, Sue Bradbury, Judy Branam, Wally Brazy, Julia Brickell, Randy Bridges, Luke Britt, Judy Brooks, Karen Boswell, Malcom Brown, Tom Bunger, Barb Cabot, Barb Campaigne, Mary Carmichael, Charles Carper, Diana Carr, Richard Carr, Jill Carraway, Boomer Christy, Bruno Civitico, Maureen Civitico, Gary Clendening, Star Cochran, Carp Combs, John Cotner, Kevin Craig, Roger Curry, Lucy Darby, Shehira Davezac, Kathy Deckard, Bob Deppe, Kevin Dukes, Sandy Duncan, Susan Eberle, Joe and Nancy Erp, Ann

Estes, Dick Ewers, Arthur Fell, Robert Fichter, Carol Fischer, John Fleener, Lee Formwalt, Justin Foster, Monroe Fritz.

Don Gest, Tom Gettinger, Margaret Gladney, Brennan Golightly, Paul Gordon, Marshall Goss, Bill Gosser, Geoff Grodner, Meg Graham, Suzanne Groennings, Ken Gros-Louis, Mary Hartman, Jim Hartman, Helen Harrell, Dean Hartley, John Hartley, Mervin Hendricks, Janet Henry, Gail Herr, Steve Higgs, Danny Higgins, Kathy Higgins, Chris Hodenfield, Steve Hofer, Catherine Hoff, Deborah Horning, John Horton, Bob Houts, Charlie Hunterman, Solomon Hursey, John Irvine, Joanne Jackson, Al Jaeger, David Johnson, Mary Johnson, Dina Kellams, Jana Kellar, Mike Kelsey, Sharon Kilgas, Al King, Teri Klassen, Dena Klein, Keith Klein, Chuck Kleinhans, Harry Koeppen, Scott Kragie, Mark Kruzan, Roger Lass, Pam Lawrence, Robert Lee, Nora Leill, Marvina Lewis, John Liu, Bill Lloyd, Vivian Lorch, Jerrold Maddox, James Madison, Andy Mahler, Bob Mann, Joan Manning, Joel Marsh, Linda Marsh, Ray Maudlin, Catherine May, Steve McClung, Monty McDaniel, Ann McGarrell, Jim McGarrell, Rachel McMasters, Bill McMillan, Ida Medlyn, Emanuel Mickel, Gail Middleton, Kathleen Mills, Conchita Mitchell, Charles Moman, Susie Moman, Jill Morris, Mike Morris, Rod Mortensen.

Ted Najam, Emily Noffke, Barbara Osipe, Jean Patteson, Ginny Peacock, Marianne Pichon, Robert Ping, Patty Pizzo, Tony Pizzo, Gary Pool, Greg Prange, Jon Pratter, Peggy Pruett, Debbie Richardson, Bruce Remak, Heidi Remak, Patricia Rhinehart, Corry Rieger, Mark Rieger, Tiiu Robison, Lynn Rockwood, Anne Rosebruck, Samuel Rosenberg, Gary Sallee, Shelley Schaap, Anne Schmitz, Bill Schrader, Phil Schrodt, Paul Schurter, Veronica Sebeok, Dan Sherman, Barbara Shoup, Tom Simes, Rick Smith, Tony Solomito, Daniel Soto, Camille Stout, Clay Stuckey, Sonya Stuckey, Bill Sturbaum, Steve Sturgeon, Abigail Sutton, Geoff Sutton, Mary Ann Sutton, Molly Sutton, Ryder Sutton, Dave Taggart, Shirley Talbot, Alan Tate, Lenny Thompson, Don Traub, Ron Unger.

Francis Valette, Vicki Vare, Martha Vicinus, Patty VanDielingen, Sally Walls, Ronald Walton, Yvette Warbonnett, Lee Ann Watson, Linda Watson, Charles Webb, Marcia Whitlow, Roy Whiteman, George Wilder, Shawn Wilson, Julia Wrubel, Nicholas Wyant, Bob Zaltsberg, Sara Zylman.

CPSIA information can be obtained
at www.ICGtesting.com
Printed in the USA
FFOW04n0300210917
40203FF

9 781457 557378